Detroit Studies in
Music Bibliography

General Editor
Bruno Nettl
University of Illinois at Urbana-Champaign

music for viola

Allegro

MICHAEL D. WILLIAMS

DETROIT STUDIES IN MUSIC BIBLIOGRAPHY NUMBER FORTY-TWO

INFORMATION COORDINATORS 1979 DETROIT

Printed and bound in the United States of America
Library of Congress Catalog Card Number 78-70022
International Standard Book Number 0-911772-95-2

Published by
Information Coordinators, Inc.
1435-37 Randolph Street
Detroit, Michigan 48226

Book design by Vincent Kibildis

CONTENTS

PREFACE

MUSIC FOR VIOLA is intended to be a source book for violists, viola teachers, librarians, and others interested in viola music. The author has attempted to locate every work for viola and to present full bibliographic information for each work. Rather than simply listing the limited information found in publications of viola music, publishers' catalogs, and many reference sources, which quite often consists only of the composer's last name, abbreviated title, and publisher, *Music for Viola* gives the following information for each work, whenever relevant (n.b., parentheses and brackets in the example below indicate that these items are enclosed in parentheses or brackets in the catalog entries).

FIRST LINE
1. Composer's full name
2. (Composer's birth and death dates)

SECOND LINE
1. Title of work
2. Larger work or collection of pieces of which this work is a part
3. Key: capital letters for major keys, lower case for minor keys
4. Opus number or other catalog number
5. (Date of composition)
6. [Instrumentation and/or alternate versions]
7. [Original instrumentation of a transcribed work]

THIRD LINE
1. An asterisk indicates that the work is currently available by purchase, rental, or loan
2. Publisher or other format (*see* List of Publishers, p. 333)
3. (Editor, arranger, or transcriber)
4. (Date of publication)
5. (r) or (loan) indicating work is available by rental or loan

Composers' names and dates have been verified in the Library of Congress *Catalog of Music and Phonorecords* and other reference sources. Work titles have been standardized since different editions of the same work often use different titles. Whenever possible, the large work or collection of which the individual work is a part has been given. In some cases, especially nineteenth-century editions, it has not been possible to secure complete information.

Instrumentation is shown, with the following exceptions:

Unaccompanied Viola: instrumentation not given; all works are for viola solo.

Viola and Keyboard: instrumentation given only if the work is for a combination other than viola and piano.

Viola and Orchestra: instrumentation given only if the work is for a combination other than viola and standard full orchestra.

Transcriptions are not listed separately. Whenever possible, the instrumentation of the source of the transcription is given. In general, works with an editor listed can be assumed to be transcriptions, even though in some cases it has been impossible to determine the original instrumentation. In the Viola and Keyboard section, the original instrumentation of concerto transcriptions is not given; the original instrumentation in these cases is viola and orchestra.

In the case of works for viola and orchestra currently available in published format, the score (often a miniature or study score) is usually available for purchase, while the parts must be rented.

The author has relied on the pioneering works of Altmann and Borissowsky, Farish, and Zeyringer (*see* Bibliography). Thanks are due to the hundreds of publishers, dealers, and individuals who provided current catalogs and other information.

My research assistant, Ms. Christanne Butler, performed her work with thoroughness and accuracy.

Preparation of *Music for Viola* has been made possible by a Research Initiation Grant and a Grant-in-Aid for Research from the University of Houston.

ABBREVIATIONS

Performance Medium

b.c.	basso continuo
bsn	bassoon
chamb ens	chamber ensemble
chamb orch	chamber orchestra
chor	chorus
clar	clarinet
Eng hn	English horn
ens	ensemble
fl	flute
guit	guitar
hn	French horn
hpscd	harpsichord
mand	mandolin
ob	oboe
orch	orchestra
org	organ
perc	percussion
pno	piano
quar	quartet
quin	quintet
rec	recorder
sax	saxophone
str	string
str bs	string bass

str orch	string orchestra
timp	timpani
trb	trombone
trp	trumpet
vl	viol
vl da gamba	viol da gamba
vla	viola
vla d'amore	viola d'amore
vlc	violoncello
vln	violin

Miscellaneous

ed.	editor, transcriber, or arranger
Ms	manuscript
orig:	original instrumentation
pub by comp	published by composer
(r)	rental
vol.	volume
*	currently available

Publishers

See List of Publishers

UNACCOMPANIED VIOLA

AGUILAR-AHUMADA, Miguel (1931-)

Piezas (3) (1957)
InstExtMus

ALLGÉN, Claude L. (1920-)

Carmen perlotense
Ms

ANGERER, Paul (1927-)

Musik (1948)
*Doblinger (1960)

ANTĨUFEEV, Boris Ivanovich (1889-)

Suite (1930)
Ms

APPLEBAUM, Samuel

The Country Fair
*Belwin-Mills
A Graceful Waltz
*Belwin-Mills
Minuets (3)
*Belwin-Mills

Souvenir
    *Belwin-Mills
Spanish Dance
    *Belwin-Mills
Waltzes (3)
    *Belwin-Mills

AREL, Bülent (1918-   )

Music (1957)
    *AmCompAll
    *Impero (1959)

ARNELL, Richard (1917-   )

Partita
    *Hinrichsen (1961)

ASAFIEV, Boris Vladimirovitch (1884-1949)

Sonata
    Musgis (1939)

BACH, Johann Sebastian (1685-1750)

Chaconne, from *Partita No. 2 in d*, BWV 1004 [orig: vln]
    *Augener (Tertis)
Fantasia Chromatica, BWV 903 [orig: hpscd]
    *Boosey (Kodály)
Siciliano
    Spratt (Cazden)
Sonata No. 1 in g, BWV 1001, and *Partita No. 1 in b*, BWV 1002 [orig: vln]
    *Peters (Forbes)
Sonatas (3) and *Partitas* (3), BWV 1001-6 [orig: vln]
    *Hofmeister (Spindler) (2 vols.)
    *International (Meyer/Vieland)
    *Pro Musica (2 vols.)
    *Ricordi (Polo)

Studies (2 vols.)
  *Hofmeister (Spindler)
Suites (6), BWV 1007-12 [orig: vlc]
  *Chester (Forbes)
  *Hofmeister (Spindler) (2 vols.)
  *International (Katims)
  International (Ritter) (4 only)
  *Leduc (Boulay)
  Pressèr (Markevitch)
  *Ricordi (Giuranna)
  Ricordi (Polo)
  *Schirmer (Lifschey)
  *Schirmer (Svecenski)
  *Sikorski (Schmidtner)

BANDINI, Bruno

  Prelude
    Ricordi

BARNES, Milton (1931-   )

  Lamentations of Jeremiah (1959)
    *Canadian (loan)

BARROWS, John Jr. (1913-   )

  Sonata (1937)
    Ms

BARTOS, Jan Zdenek (1908-   )

  Partita, Op. 36 (1944)
    pub by comp

BAUR, Jürg (1918-   )

  Sonata
    *Breitkopf

BECERRA SCHMIDT, Gustavo (1925-   )

Partita (1961)
Ms

BENTZON, Jørgen Liebenberg (1897-1951)

Fabula, Op. 42
Skandinavisk

BEREND, Giltay (1910-   )

Studi concertanti
Donemus

BERGER, Melvin

Fourteenth-Century Dances (3) [vla, with tambour ad lib]
*MCA

BERIO, Luciano (1925-   )

Sequenza VI (1969)
*Universal

BERNAUD, Alain

Contrastes
*Rideau

BEYER, Frank Michael (1928-   )

Cadenzas to Viola Concerti by Hoffmeister, K. Stamitz, Zelter
*Eulenburg

BIBER, Heinrich Ignaz Franz von (1644-1704)

Passacaglia [orig: vln]
*Chester (Rostal)

BLACKWOOD, Easley (1933-   )

> *Sonata*
> *Elkan-Vogel

BLANK, Allan (1925-   )

> *A Song of Ascents*
> *Okra
> *Seesaw

BLOCH, Ernest (1880-1959)

> *Suite* (1958)
> *BroudeBr

BLOCK, Robert Paul

> *Fantasy* (1967; rev. 1973)
> *MusRara (1974)

BOHNKE, Emil (1888-1928)

> *Sonata No. 2*, Op. 13
> Simrock (1925)

BONSEL, Adriaan (1918-   )

> *Elegy*
> *Donemus

BOŘKOVEČ, Pavel (1894-1972)

> *Sonata in C*, Op. 12
> Hudebni (1933)

BORNOFF, [?]

> *Fiddler's Holiday* [vla or vla, pno]
> *Fischer

Violin Sings [vla or vla, pno]
  *Fischer

BOURGUIGNON, Francis de (1890-1961)

  Suite
    Ms

BOURNONVILLE, Armand

  Appassionato
    *Billaudot

BOZZA, Eugene Joseph (1905-   )

  Parthie
    *Leduc

BRAUN, Jehezkiel (1922-   )

  Jester's Lament
    *IsMusInst

BRÜN, Herbert (1918-   )

  Sonatina
    *IsMusPub (Golan) (1954)

BRUNI, Antonio Bartolomeo (1751-1821)

  Sonatas (3), Op. 27
    Sieber

BRUNSWICK, Mark (1902-1971)

  Fantasia (1933)
    *NewValley

BURKHARD, Willy (1900-1955)

> *Sonata*, Op. 59
> > *Bärenreiter (1958)

BUSCH, Adolf Georg Wilhelm (1891-1952)

> *Suite*, Op. 16a
> > Ms

CAGE, John (1912-)

> *59½" for a String Player* (1953)
> > *Peters

CAMPAGNOLI, Bartolomeo (1751-1827)

> *Caprices* (41), Op. 22
> > Augener (Kreuz)
> > *Breitkopf
> > *International (Primrose)
> > *Peters (Sitt)
> > *Ricordi (Consolini)
> > *Schirmer (Lifschey)
> > *Sikorski (Schmidtner) (24 only)
> *Divertimenti* (7), Op. 18 [orig: vln]
> > *Hofmeister (Spindler)

CAZDEN, Norman (1914-)

> *Chamber Sonata No. 2*
> > pub by comp
> *Concerto for Ten Instruments*, Op. 10 (4th movement)
> > *MCA
> *Sonata*, Op. 17, No. 2
> > AmCompAll
> > *Andrews

CHAILLEY, Jacques (1910-)

 Cadenzas for Mozart Sinfonia Concertante, K. 364
  *Leduc

CHILDS, Robert Barney (1926-)

 Music for One Player
  *AmCompAll
 Sonata
  *AmCompAll

COOLEY, Carlton (1898-)

 Etude Suite
  *ElkanH

CRESTON, Paul (1906-)

 Suite, Op. 13 (1937)
  *Shawnee

DAVID, Hans Theodore (1902-)

 Sonata
  pub by comp

DAVID, Johann Nepomuk (1895-)

 Sonata, Op. 31, No. 3 (1943)
  *Breitkopf (1947)

DAWSON, Ted

 Chameleon (1974)
  *Canadian (loan)

DEGEN, Helmuth (1911-)

 Piece, from *Die grosse Reihe*
  *Müller (1954)

DIETHELM, Caspar (1926-)

 Sonatas No. 1, Op. 118 (1974) and *No. 2*, Op. 121
  *Amadeus (1975)

DONATONI, Franco (1927-)

 Sonata
  Drago

DORSON, C.

 La Chanson du vent
  Deiss (1922)

DRIESSLER, Johannes (1921-)

 Sonata (1946)
  Hinnenthal (1948)

DRUSCHININ, F.

 Sonata (1961)
  Ms

DUKE, John Woods (1899-)

 Suite (1944)
  *NewValley

EBEL VON SOSEN, Otto (1899-)

 Arioso im alten Stil
  Peters

EGGERMANN, Fritz (1898-)

> *Interpolations*
> > Ms

EISMA, Will (1929-)

> *Non-lecture Ill*
> > *Donemus

ELLING, H

> *Elegy*
> > pub by comp (ca. 1930)

ENGELMANN, Johannes (1890-1945)

> *Trauer-Sonata in c*, Op. 41
> > Breitkopf (1932)

EPSTEIN, David M. (1930-)

> *Fantasy Variations*
> > *MCA (1971)

ERSFELD, Christian

> *Ständchen*, Op. 10 [orig: vln, pno]
> > Simon (Ritter)

ESCHER, Peter Alfred (1915-)

> *Musica*, Op. 65
> > Ms

FERRAGUZZI, Renzo (1915-)

> *Stampa* (1940)
> > Ms

FERRITTO, John

> *Canzone*, Op. 8
>> *AmCompAll

FODI, John

> *Divisions III* (1971)
>> *Canadian (loan)

FORTNER, Wolfgang (1907-)

> *Aria*
>> Ms

FRANCO, Johan H. G. (1908-)

> *Sonata*
>> *AmCompAll

FRANKEL, Benjamin (1906-1973)

> *Sonata*, Op. 7
>> Ms

FRANKEN, Wim (1922-)

> *Sonata* (1948)
>> *Donemus (1950)

FRICKER, Peter Racine (1920-)

> *Movements* (3), Op. 25
>> pub by comp (1955)

FUCHS, Lillian

> *Fantasy Etudes*
>> *Colombo

Sonata Pastorale
  *Associated (1956)
12 Caprices
  Schirmer (1950)

FULKERSON, James (1945-)

Patterns V
  *Moderne

GARBE, F.

Pieces (4), Op. 1
  SchmidtCF (1889)

GEIER, Oscar (1889-)

Suite, Op. 15, No. 1
  *Hofmeister (Spindler)

GEISSLER, Fritz (1921-)

Sonata
  *Hofmeister

GELBRUN, Artur (1913-)

Pieces (5)
  *IsMusInst

GENZMER, Harald (1909-)

Sonata (1957)
  Litolff (1958)
  *Peters

GIBBONS, Orlando (1583-1625)

> *Fantasias* (6), 2 vols. [orig: viol]
> *Peters (Mueller)

GIUCCI, Carlos (1904-1958)

> *Preludio y Movimiento Fugado Núm 1* (ca. 1950)
> Ms

GOLEMINOV, Marin Petrov (1908-)

> *Kleine Suite*
> Bulgarischer (1956)

GORECKI, Henryk Mikolaj (1933-)

> *La Musiquette*, Op. 25
> *PolWydMuz

GRAINGER, Percy Aldridge (1882-1961)

> *Arrival Platform* (Room Music No. 7)
> *Schott
> *Sussey Mummer's Christmas Carol*
> Ms

GRÖNING, Herbert

> *Kleine Stücke* (1948)
> Moeck (1950)

GROSS, Robert

> *Sonatina*
> *AmCompAll

HAMPE, Charlotte (1910-)

Short Baroque Dances (7)
  *Ries & Erler (1937)

HANESYAN, Harutyun

Cadenza for Telemann Concerto in D
  *Eschig
Cadenza to F. A. Hofmeister Concerto in D
  *Eschig
Cadenzas for the Handel Concerto in b and *Telemann Concerto in G*
  *Eschig
Cadenzas to Stamitz Concerto in D
  *Eschig
Cadenzas to Zelter Concerto in E-flat and *Dittersdorf Concerto in F*
  *Eschig

HARTZELL, Eugene (1932-)

Monologue 7. Excursions (1969)
  *Doblinger (1972)

HEKSTER, Walter

Occurence
  *Donemus

HERBERGER, Rolf

Sonata (1961)
  Ms

HEROLD, Jiři (1875- ?)

Piece
  Hudebni

HESS, Ernst (1912-1968)

> *Suite*, Op. 14 (1936)
> Ms

HESS, Willy (1906-)

> *Sonata*, Op. 77
> *Amadeus (1973)
> *Eulenburg

HÉTU, Jacques (1938-)

> *Variations*, Op. 11 [vla or vln or vlc]
> *Canadian

HINDEMITH, Paul (1895-1963)

> *Sonata*, Op. 11, No. 5 (1923)
> *Schott
> *Sonata*, Op. 25, No. 1 (1923)
> *Schott
> *Sonata*, Op. 31, No. 2 (1924)
> *Schott

HOESL, Albert

> *Suite*
> Cor

HOVHANESS, Alan (1911-)

> *Chahagir*, Op. 56a
> *Rongwen

HUEBER, Kurt Anton (1928-)

> *Sonata*, Op. 4
> *Heinrichshofen

HÜBNER, Johann (1888-   )

> *Suite*, Op. 17 (1915)
> Ms

HUMEL, Gerald (1931-   )

> *Sonata No. 1* (1963)
> *Bote&Bock

IRINO, Yoshiro (1921-   )

> *Suite* (1971)
> Ms

JEMNITZ, Alexander (1890-   )

> *Sonata*, Op. 46
> Kultura
> Rozsavölgyi (1941)

JEMNITZ, Sándor (1899-1963)

> *Sonata*, Op. 46
> *Budapest

JESINGHAUS, Walter (1902-1966)

> *Sonatina nostalgica*
> Ms

JOHNSON, Thomas Arnold (1908-   )

> *Action Music IV*
> *Associated

JOLIVET, André (1905-   )

> *Eglogues* (5)
> *Billaudot

JONES, Charles (1910-)
   Threemody (1947)
      Ms

KAMINSKI, Heinrich (1886-1946)
   Prelude and Fugue in C
      *Peters (Kromer) (1936)

KAUDER, Hugo (1888-)
   Kleine Suite in a
      Universal (1926)

KELLY, Robert (1916-)
   Suite [vla or vlc]
      *AmCompAll

KREJČI, Miroslav (1891-1964)
   Mala Suita
      Verband

KRENEK, Ernst (1900-)
   Sonata, Op. 92, No. 3 (1942)
      *Bomart (1954)

KURTÁG, György (1926-)
   Signs, Op. 5
      *Budapest

LAKNER, Yehoshua (1924-)
   Improvisation
      *IsMusPub (1958)

LEHMANN, Hans Ulrich (1937-   )

> *Studies*
> > *Ars Viva
> > Schott

LEMBERGER, Karl

> *Andante in g with 5 Variations* (1948)
> > *Hieber

LEMELAND, Aubert

> *Sonata*, Op. 7
> > *Jobert (1970)

LEVITIN, Yuri Abramovitch (1912-   )

> *Variations*
> > MezhdKniga

LÉVY, Ernst (1895-   )

> *Suite*
> > Ms

LEVY, Frank (1930-   )

> *Sonata*
> > Cor

LIDOV, David

> *Fantasy* (1964)
> > *Canadian (loan)

LITINSZKY, Heinrich

> *Sonata*
>> RussSt (1933)
>> Universal

LOEB, David

> *Intermezzi* (2)
>> *Branch
> *Sonata No. 2*
>> *Branch
> *Sonata No. 3*
>> *Branch
> *Sonata No. 6*
>> *Branch
> *Suite*
>> *Branch

LORENZITI, Bernard

> *Sonatas*, Op. 39
>> Davie

LUENING, Otto (1900-)

> *Sonata* (1958)
>> AmCompAll

LUTYENS, Elisabeth Agnes (1906-)

> *Sonata*, Op. 5, No. 4 (1938)
>> Lengnick (1946)

MACBRIDE, David

> *Alone Together* (1)
>> *Seesaw

MACONCHY, Elizabeth (1907-   )

Pieces (5) (1937)
Ms

MALOOF, William

Prelude and Chaconne
*Boston

MANNINO, Franco (1924-   )

Sonata
*Curci

MARCEL, Luc-André (1919-   )

Sonata
Transatlantiques

MARCKHL, Erich (1902-   )

Sonata (1948)
Ms

MASSIAS, Gérard (1933-   )

Douze etudes en trois suites
*Jobert

MATSUBA, Ryo

Albumblatt
Ms

MATYS, Jiři (1927-   )

Sonata
Ms

MAZAS, Jacque Féréol (1782-1849)

Mélodies faciles (8) [orig: vln]
Bellmann (Pagels)

MÉTRAL, Pierre

Arabesque, from *Disparatès*
*Tonos

MEYER, Karl Walter (1902-)

Music (1930)
Ms

MITREA-CILARIANU, Mihai G. (1935-)

Glose
*Salabert (1969)

MOLLICONE, Henry

Chaunt
*AmCompAll

MOSSOLOV, Alexander Vassilievich (1900-)

Sonata (1930)
Ms

NOBRE, Marlos (1939-)

Sonata, Op. 11 (1963)
*SDMBrazil
*Tonos

ORGAD, Ben-Zion (1926-)

Monologue
*IsMusPub

PAGANINI, Niccolò (1782-1840)

> *Caprices* (24), Op. 1 [orig: vln]
> > *International (Raby)
> > *Ricordi (Ferraguzzi) (6 only)

PAISIELLO, Giovanni (1740-1816)

> *Variations*
> > Pleyel

PALS, Leopold van der (1884-)

> *Sonata*
> > Ms

PASCAL, Léon

> *Divertissements* (25)
> > *Heugel

PAUER, Jiři (1919-)

> *Sonata in Quarter-tones*
> > Ms

PENN, William A.

> *Guernica*
> > *Seesaw

PENTLAND, Barbara (1912-)

> *Variations* (1965)
> > *Canadian (loan)

PERLE, George (1915-)

> *Sonata* (1942)
> > *EdCoopIntAm

Sonata, Op. 12 (1944)
Ms

PERSICHETTI, Vincent (1915-)

Infanta Marina
*Elkan-Vogel

PISK, Paul Amadeus (1893-)

Sonata (1925)
Ms

POCHON, Alfred (1878-1959)

Passacaglia (1942)
Foetisch

POLIN, Claire J. (1926-)

Serpentine
*Seesaw

POLO, Enrico (1868- ?)

Partita in B-flat
Suvini-Zerboni (1950)
Sonata in D
Suvini-Zerboni
Sonata in e
Suvini-Zerboni (1950)
Studi-Sonate (3)
Suvini-Zerboni

PORTER, Quincy (1897-1966)

Poem, Speed Etude
AmCompAll

Suite (1930)
    InstIntMus (1942)
    Valley

RAPHAEL, Günter Albert Rudolf (1903-1960)

Sonata in c, Op. 7, No. 1
    Breitkopf (1925)
Sonatas in G and *e*, Op. 46, Nos. 3 and 4
    Müller (1960)

REGER, Max (1873-1916)

Suites (3) in *g*, *D*, and *e*, Op. 131d
    *International
    *Peters (Hermann) (1952)

REINHARDT, Bruno (1929-)

Fantasy
    *OR-TAV

REUTER, Hermann (1900-)

Cinco caprichos sobre Cervantes
    *Schott

RICHTER, Marga (1926-)

Suite
    *Branch

RIELY, Dennis (1943-)

Variations III
    *Peters (1973)

RIVILIS, P. 7000516

Sonata
Ms

ROGER, Kurt George (1895-1966)

Sonata, Op. 79 (1954)
Ms

ROIKJER, Kjell (1901-)

Introduktion og Tema med Variationer
*Skandinavisk

ROLLA, Antonio (1798-1837)

Idylls (6)
André (1861)
Musicus

RUBBRA, Edmund Duncan (1901-)

Meditations on a Byzantine Hymn, *"O Quando in Cruce,"* Op. 117
*Lengnick

SALMENHAARA, Erkki (1941-)

Elegia No. 4
*Fazer

SCHER, V.

Sonata
MezhdKniga (Kramarov)

SCHIBLER, Armin (1920-)

Kleines Konzert
Ahn&Sim (1956)

SCHNEIDER, Georg Abraham (1770-1839)

> *Solos* (6), Op. 19
>> Breitkopf
>> Pleyel

SCHROEDER, Hermann (1904-   )

> *Music in 5 Movements*
>> *Lienau (1955)
> *Sonata* (1974)
>> *Gerig

SCHUMANN, Robert Alexander (1810-1856)

> *Solo*, from *Manfred*, Op. 115 [orig: Eng hn]
>> Fromont (Dumas)

SEAR, Walter Edmond (1930-   )

> *Sonata*
>> Ms

SEHLBACH, Erich Oswald (1898-   )

> *Music*, Op. 87, No. 1
>> *Möseler

SEREBRIER, Jose (1938-   )

> *Sonata*
>> *Peer-Southern

SHER, Veniamin Iosifovich (1900-1962)

> *Sonata*
>> *MezhdKniga (Kramarov)

SHULMAN, Alan (1915-)

Suite
*Templeton

SICCARDI, Honorio (1897-)

Sonata
Ms

SILVERMAN, Faye-Ellen

Memories
*Seesaw

SIMBRIGER, Heinrich (1904-)

Suite, Op. 26
Kahnt (1941)

ŠLIK, Miroslav (1898-)

Sonata Macedonika
Ms

SMITH, Leland (1925-)

Suite
*AmCompAll

SODDERLAND, Jan (1903-)

Suite
Donemus (1948)

SOULAGE, Marcelle Fanny Henriette (1894-)

Sonata in F, Op. 43
Buffet (1930)

STADLMAIR, Hans (1929-   )

Sonata (1960)
  *Breitkopf (1961)

STEIN, Leon (1910-   )

Sonata
  *AmCompAll

STERANS, Peter Pindar (1931-   )

Variations
  *AmCompAll

STOCKHAUSEN, Karlheinz (1928-   )

From the 7 Days
  *Universal
Plus Minus
  *Universal

STRAVINSKY, Igor (1882-1971)

Élégie (1944)
  *Associated
   Chappell (1945)
  *Schott (1945)

STUTCHEVSKY, Joachim Yehoyachin (1891-   )

Soliloquia
  *OR-TAV

TATE, Phyllis (1911-   )
Variegations
  *Oxford (1972)

TELEMANN, Georg Philipp (1681-1767)

Fantasias (12), 2 vols. [orig: vln]
  *McGinnis (Rood)

TOCH, Ernst (1887-1964)

Impromptus (3), Op. 90
Mills

TOEBOSCH, Louis (1916-)

Toccata, aria e finale, Op. 102
*Donemus (1974)

TREUTLER, Paul (1896-)

Suite (1930)
Ms

TUROK, Paul H. (1929-)

Sonata
*Seesaw

VAČKÁŘ, Dalibor Cyril (1906-)

Dialogy
*Panton

VAN DE VATE, Nancy (1931-)

Etudes (6)
*ManuscriptPub

VOLPERT, Andreas (1918-)

Suite, Op. 11
*Hieber (Ackermann) (1954)

VOSS, Friedrich (1930-)

Variations (1962-1963)
*Breitkopf (1964)

VYCPÁLEK, Ladislav (1882-1969)

> *Suite*, Op. 21
>> Artia
>> Schott (1930)

WACHS, J.

> *Variations on an Ukrainian Theme* (ca. 1950)
>> Ms

WALLACE, William Vincent (1812-1865)

> *Heortasis*
>> *Canadian (loan)

WASHBURN, Gary

> *The Breathless Feather*
>> *Seesaw

WEINER, Stanley Milton (1925-   )

> *Sonata*, Op. 17
>> *MCA (1971)

WELLESZ, Egon Joseph (1885-1974)

> *Präludium*, Op. 112
>> *Doblinger
> *Rhapsody*, Op. 87
>> *Doblinger

WIÉNER, Jean (1896-   )

> *Sonata in D*
>> *Choudens

WIGY, F.

Sonata
Maurer (1956)

WILLAUME, G.

La Noce bretonne (1906)
DuWast

WILLIAMSON, Malcolm (1931-)

Partita on Themes of Walton
*Weinberger

WINDSPERGER, Lothar (1885-1935)

Ode in C, Op. 15, No. 2
Schott (1919)
Sonata, Op. 42
Schott (1930)

WOLPE, Stefan (1902-1972)

Piece No. 2 [orig: vln]
*McGinnis (Perrin) (1970)

WYMAN, Dann

Aloneness
*Seesaw

YSAŸE, Eugène (1858-1931)

Cadenzas for Mozart Sinfonia Concertante
*Ysaÿe

ZIMMERMANN, Bernd Alois (1918-1970)

    Sonata (1955)
      *Schott (1956)

ZONN, Paul (1938-)

    Sonata
      *AmCompAll

Anthologies

ERRANTE, Belisario, ed.

    Viola Player's Solo Album
      *Shawnee

MEYER, Clemens, ed.

    Solobuch. Sammlung ausgewählter Solowerke, 2 vols.
      Benjamin (1899, 1900)

PAGELS, Louis, ed.

    Solobuch. 31 Konzert-u. Vortragsstücke revidiert u. bezeichnet
      Oertel (1896)
    Solobuch. Sammlung beliebtester klassischer und neuer moderner Vortragsstücke
      SchmidtCF (1898)

REICHENBACH, T. Hermann, ed.

    Mein Gambenbuch, Spielmusik [vla or vl da gamba]
      Kallmeyer (Jöde) (1922)

VIOLA WITH KEYBOARD

ABENDROTH, Walter (1896-)

Sonata No. 1 in G, Op. 21a
  *Müller (1956)
Sonata No. 2 in C, Op. 21b
  *Müller (1957)

ABSIL, Jean (1893-)

Concerto, Op. 54
  *Belgian

ACCOLAY, J. B. (1845-1910)

Concerto No. 1 [orig: vln, orch]
  *Schirmer (Doty)

ACHRON, Joseph (1886-1943)

Pieces (2), Op. 65
  *IsMusPub

ADAM, Adolphe Charles (1803-1856)

Pas de deux, from *Giselle* [orig: orch]
  Seeling (ca. 1880)

ADAMS, Charles E.

Pieces (7)
  Breitkopf (1911)

ADKINS, Greg

Pastorale
    *Ludwig

ADLER, Samuel H. (1928-   )

Song and Dance [orig: vla, orch]
    *Oxford

ADOLPHUS, Milton (1913-   )

Improvisation, Op. 61
    *AmCompAll

AGUIRRE, Julián (1869-1924)

Huella [orig: pno]
    *Fischer (Heifetz/Primrose)

AHRENS, Joseph (1904-   )

Sonata [vla, org]
    *Müller

AKIMENKO, Fyodor Stepanovitch (1876-1945)

Romance
        Belaieff
        Bessel (1926)

ALBÉNIZ, Isaac Manuel Francisco (1860-1909)

L'Automne, from *Les Saisons* [orig: pno]
        Costallat
        *Leduc
Mallorca: Barcarola, Op. 202 [orig: pno]
        *UnMusEsp (Amaz)
Puerta de tierra: Bolero, from *Recuerdos de Viaje* [orig: pno]
        *UnMusEsp (Amaz)

Tango in D [orig: pno]
*Oxford (Forbes)

ALBIN, Roger (1920-)

Tre pezzi pazzi [orig: vla, orch]
*Rideau

ALBRECHT, Alexander (1885-)

Suite concertante
*Slovenský

ALETTER, William

Mélodie
*Fischer (Buechner)
Petite gavotte
*Fischer (Deery)

ALKAN, Charles Henri Valentin (1813-1888)

Grande sonate, Op. 47
Costallat

ALLEN, Herbert Philipp

Sonata in d
Rushworth (1936)

ALLGÉN, Claude L. (1920-)

Dradkans
Svenska

AMES, William

Sonata
*AmCompAll

AMIROV, Fikret (1922-   )

Elegy
  *MezhdKniga (Anshelevich)
  Musgis (1951)

AMRAM, David Werner (1930-   )

The Wind and the Rain
  *Peters

ANDERSEN, Karl (1903-   )

Der Fiedeltrick (En Spillemanstubb)
  Hansen

ANDERSON, Kenneth

Diversions (3)
  *Bosworth

ANDERSON, M. Bradford

Prelude in Canon [vla, pno or hn, pno]
  *Boosey (1973)

ANDERSSON, William Robert

Diversions (3)
  Bosworth

ANDERTON, Howard Orsmond (1861-1934)

Lyrics (2)
  Swan (1923)

ANDRIESSEN, Hendrik (1892-   )

Sonata
  *Donemus

ANGERER, Paul (1927-)

Concerto (1962)
*Doblinger
Ruminatio (1953)
pub by comp

[Anonymous]

Sonata in B-flat [vla, hpscd]
Breitkopf (1762)
Sonata in G [vla, hpscd]
Breitkopf (1762)
Sonata in G [vla, hpscd]
Breitkopf (1762)
Sonatas (3) in *C*, *D*, and *G* (ca. 1700)
Doblinger (Sabatini) (1960)

ANTIUFEEV, Boris Ivanovich (1889-)

Concerto, Op. 45
*MezhdKniga
Dramatic Fragments (2), Op. 40
Musgis (1946)
Romance and Scherzo, Op. 18
Ms
Sonata (1926)
Ms

ANTUNES, Jorge (1942-)

Microformóbiles I (1970)
Suvini-Zerboni

APPLEBAUM, Edward

Foci
*Chester

ARDÉVOL, José (1911-   )

Sonatina (1932)
Ms

AREL, Bülent (1918-   )

Sonatina
Ms

ARENDS, H.

Ballade, Op. 4
Greiner (ca. 1884)

ARIOSTI, Attilio Malachia (1666-1740?)

Lezione (Sonatas) (6), *in E-flat, A, e, F, e,* and *D*   [orig: vla d'amore, b.c.]
Hill (Piatti/Marchet)
*Santis (Sabatini)
Schott (Piatti/Marchet) (1912)
Sonata No. 2 in A   [orig: vla d'amore, b.c.]
Durand (Waelfelghem)
Sonata No. 6 in D   [orig: vla d'amore, b.c.]
Schirmer (Piatti)
Sonatas (2) *in e* and *C*   [orig: vla d'amore, b.c.]
*Schott (Klein/Weiss)
Stockholm Sonatas   [orig: vla d'amore, b.c.]
*Bärenreiter (Weiss)

ARISTAKESIAN, Emin Aspetovich

Concerto
*MezhdKniga

ARMA, Paul (1905-   )

Divertimento No. 4 in B-flat
Lemoine (1956)

ARNE, Thomas Augustine (1710-1778)

Sonata in B-flat
 *Oxford (Craxton)

ARNOLD, Malcolm Henry (1921-)

Sonata, Op. 17
 *Lengnick (1948)

ARNOLD, R. P.

Elegia
 Breitkopf (1903)

ASHTON, Algernon (1859-1937)

Ländler
 Stainer
Sonata in a, Op. 44
 Simrock (1891)
Tarantella
 Stainer

ATTERBERG, Kurt (1887-1974)

Sonata, Op. 27
 Nordiska

ATTERN, Wilhelm

Variations and Rondo on a Theme from *La dame blanche* by Boieldieu, Op. 2
 Langewiesche (1835)

AUMILLER, A. de

Melodia
 Ricordi (ca. 1860)

AVSHALOMOFF, Jacob (1919-   )

Bagatelles (2)
   Mercury
Evocations
   *AmCompAll
Sonata
   MusPress
Sonatine (1947)
   *Mercury

BABBITT, Milton (1916-   )

Composition (1950)
   Bomart
   *Peters

BACEWICZ, Grázyna (1913-1969)

Concerto
   *PolWydMuz/Curci

BACH, Carl Philipp Emanuel (1714-1788)

Concerto in a, Wq 170 (1750) [orig: vlc, orch]
   *Leduc (R. Boulay/L. Boulay)
Concerto in B-flat, Wq 171 (1751) [orig: vlc, orch]
   *Breitkopf (Klengel)
Solfeggietto, Wq 117 [orig: hpscd]
   *Fischer (Primrose)
Sonata in g, Wq 88 [vla, hpscd]
   Bisping (Stephan)
   *International (Primrose)
   *Schott (Ruf)

BACH, Johann Christian (1735-1782)

Concerto in B-flat [orig: bsn, orch]
   *Billaudot (Massis)

Concerto in c
    *Salabert (Casadesus)
    Schirmer

BACH, Johann Christoph Friedrich (1732-1795)

Concerto in E-flat
    *Bote&Bock (Seiler/Kübart/Roetscher) (vla, 2 pnos)
Lament
    Musicus

BACH, Johann Sebastian (1685-1750)

Adagio
    Concert (Grant)
Adagio, from *Organ Concerto No. 3 in a* (after Vivaldi), BWV 593 [orig:
    Bach—org; Vivaldi—2 vlns, orch]
    *International (Borisovsky)
Adagio, from *Toccata and Fugue*
    Boosey (Tertis)
Adagio, from *Toccata in C*, BWV 564 [orig: org]
    *Fischer (Siloti/Tertis)
Air, from *Christmas Oratorio*, BWV 248
    Salabert (Alexanian)
Air, from *Suite No. 3 in D*, BWV 1068 [orig: orch]
    *Fischer (Wilhelmj/Pagels/Perlman)
Air and Gavotte, from *Suite No. 6 in D*, BWV 1012 [orig: vlc]
    *Schott (Ries)
    *Williams (Tolhurst)
All Glory Be to God on High
    Oxford (Forbes/Richardson)
Andante
    Curwen
Andante, from *Italian Concerto*, BWV 971 [orig: hpscd]
    *Eschig (Ronchini)
Arioso, from *Cantata No. 156* [Sinfonia] and *Clavier Concerto in f*,
    BWV 1056 [Largo]
    *Concert (Grant)
    *Fischer (Isaac)

Begluckte Herde
   Oxford (Hamilton)
Bourrée
   Williams (Browne)
Chorale Preludes (3) [orig: org]
   Oxford (Forbes)
Come, Redeemer of Our Race
   *Oxford (Forbes/Richardson)
Concerto in D, BWV 1043 [orig: 2 vlns, orch]
   Boosey (Tertis)
Fantasie courante, from *English Suite No. 4 in F*, BWV 809 [orig: hpscd]
   *ElkanH (Courte)
Gavotte, from *French Suite No. 6 in E*, BWV 817 [orig: hpscd]
   *Augener
Gavotte in A
   Oxford (Forbes)
I Call to Thee
   Oxford (Templeton)
It Is Finished
   *Spratt (Krane)
Jesu, Joy of Man's Desiring
   *Oxford (Forbes)
Komm, süsser Tod, BWV 478 [orig: SATB]
   *Schott (Tertis)
Largo, from *Cantata No. 106*
   *Ricordi (Janigro)
Little Classics (10)
   *Fischer (Murphy)
Lord Jesus Christ, Be Present Now, BWV 332 [orig: SATB]
   Oxford (Forbes/Richardson)
Polonaise in B-flat, from *French Suite No. 6*, BWV 817 [orig: hpscd]
   Peters (Klengel)
Prelude
   Boosey
Prelude and Gigue
   Sprague-Coleman (Cooley)
Prelude in A
   Oxford (Forbes)
Sheep May Safely Graze
   *Oxford (Forbes)

Siciliano
>Spratt (Cazden)

Sinfonia, from *Cantata No. 156*
>Oxford (Forbes)

Sonata in F, BWV 1022 [orig: vln, hpscd]
>*Peters (Forbes)

Sonatas (3) in *G, D*, and *g*, BWV 1027-29 [orig: vl da gamba, hpscd]
>*Breitkopf (Naumann)
>*International (Naumann)
>*Peters (Forbes)
>*Ricordi (Consolini)

Sonatas (3) and *Partitas* (3), BWV 1001-6 [orig: vln]
>Breitkopf
>*International (David/Hermann) (2 vols.)

Suite No. 1 in G, BWV 1007 (3 mvts. only) [orig: vlc]
>Lengnick (Johnson)

BACH, P. D. Q. *See* **Schickele, Peter**

BACH, Wilhelm Friedemann (1710-1784)

Sonata in c [vla, pno or vla, hpscd] [J. G. Graun?]
>*Oxford (Pessl)

BACHELET, Alfred (1864-1944)

Barcarolle, nocturne et petite histoire
>Durand

BACICH, Anthony

Tone Poems
>Willis

BACIN, [?]

Serenade
>Peters

BACON, Ernst (1898-   )

Koschatiana
    *MCA
Suite
    Ms

BADINGS, (Henk) Hendrik Herman (1907-   )

Cavatina (1952)
    *Donemus
Quempas [vla, org]
    *Donemus
Sonata (1951)
    *Donemus (1951)

BÄCK, Sven-Erik (1919-   )

Elegy
    *Hansen

BAERVOETS, Raymond (1930-   )

Rhapsodie
    *Metropolis

BAEYENS, August Louis (1895-1966)

Concerto, Op. 54 (1956)
    *Metropolis

BAKALEINIKOV, Vladimir Romanovitch (1885-1953)

Aria (1935)
    Ms

BAKER, Michael

Counterplay (1973) [orig: vla, str orch]
    *Canadian (loan)

BAKLANOVA, Natal'ia Vladimirovna

Russian Folk Song: The Spinning Wheel
*MezhdKniga

BANCQUART, Alain (1934-)

Concerto
*Jobert

BANTOCK, Sir Granville (1868-1946)

Salve Regina
Chester (ca. 1925)
Sonata in F (1920)
*Chester (1920)

BARATI, George (1913-)

Cantabile e ritmico (1947)
*Peer-Southern (1954)

BARBIER, René (1890-)

Sonata, Op. 12
*Belgian

BARGIEL, Woldemar (1828-1897)

Adagio, Op. 38 [orig: vla, orch or vlc, orch]
Associated

BARLOW, David Frederick Rothwell (1927-)

Siciliano
*Novello

BARNETT, David (1907-   )

Ballade, Op. 16
*Oxford (Primrose)

BARTH, Rudolf

Sonata in F, Op. 7 [orig: vlc, pno]
Rieter (1883)

BARTÓK, Béla (1881-1945)

Concerto (1945)
*Boosey (Serly)
Contrasts [orig: vln, clar, pno]
Boosey (1952)
An Evening in the Village
*Budapest (Vaczay)
Kultura

BARTOŠ, Jan Zdeněk (1908-   )

Sonatine, Op. 46
*Artia
Orbis (Hyska/Berkovec) (1950)
Statni (Hyska)

BARTOŠ, Josef (1887-   )

Sonatina
Panton (r)

BASSETT, Leslie Raymond (1923-   )

Sonata
*AmCompAll

BATE, Stanley Richard (1911-1959)

> *Pastorale*, Op. 57
> > Ms

BAUER, Marion (1887-1955)

> *Sonata* (1936) [vla, pno or clar, pno]
> > *SPAM
> *Sonata*, Op. 22
> > Schirmer (1951)

BAUMANN, Paul (1903-)

> *Sonata*
> > Ms

BAX, Arnold Edward Trevor (1883-1953)

> *Legend* (1929)
> > Murdoch (1930)
> *Phantasy* [orig: vla, orch]
> > Murdoch
> *Sonata in G*
> > Murdoch (1925)

BAXENDALE, Christabell (1886-)

> *Plaintive Melody*
> > *Bosworth

BAZELAIRE, Paul (1886-)

> *Funerailles*, Op. 120
> > Salabert

BEALE, James MacArthur (1924-)

> *Ballade*, Op. 23
> > *Am CompAll

BECERRA SCHMIDT, Gustavo (1925-   )

Sonata (1958)
    InstExtMus

BECK, Conrad Arthur (1901-   )

Concerto
    Schirmer
    *Schott (1952)

BECKER, Fritz

Charakterstücke (3), Op. 16
    Kistner (1897)

BEESON, Jack (1921-   )

Sonata
    Ms

BEETHOVEN, Ludwig van (1770-1827)

Alla Polacca, from *Serenade in D*, Op. 8 [orig: vln, vla, vlc]
    *Oxford (Forbes)
Country Dances [orig: orch]
    *Oxford (Forbes/Richardson)
Grand Duo, from *Septet in E-flat*, Op. 20
    Peters (Hermann)
Menuetto, from *Sonata in E-flat*, Op. 31, No. 3 [orig: pno]
    Cramer (Jacobson)
Notturno in D, Op. 42 [based on Serenade in D, Op. 8; arr. by Beethoven]
    *Schott (Primrose)
Pieces (2), WoO 43: No. 1, *Sonatina in c* [orig: mand, hpscd]
    Oxford (Forbes)
Romance in F, Op. 50 [orig: vln, orch]
    *Augener
Romances (2) in *G*, Op. 40, and *F*, Op. 50 [orig: vln, orch]
    *International
    *Peters (Hermann)

Rondo in G, WoO 41 [orig: vln, pno]
   *Schott (Forbes)
Sonata in A, Op. 69 [orig: vlc, pno]
   *International
Sonata in F, Op. 17 [orig: hn, pno]
   *International
Sonata in F, Op. 24 ("Spring") [orig: vln, pno]
   *Peters (Forbes)
Sonata in g, Op. 5, No. 2 [orig: vlc, pno]
   *Augener (Tertis)
   *International
Sonatas (5) in *F*, Op. 5, No. 1; in *g*, Op. 5, No. 2; in *A*, Op. 69; in *C*,
   Op. 102, No. 1; in *D*, Op. 102, No. 2 [orig: vlc, pno]
   Breitkopf (Naumann)
Variations in E-flat on Mozart's "Bei Männern, welche Liebe fühlen,"
   from *Die Zauberflöte*, WoO 46 [orig: vlc, pno]
   International
   *Peters (Forbes)
Variations (12) *in F* on Mozart's "Ein Mädchen oder Weibchen," from
   Die Zauberflöte, Op. 66 [orig: vlc, pno]
   Boosey (Tertis)
Zärtliche Liebe, WoO 123 [orig: voice, pno]
   Schott (Moffat) (1930)

BEHRENS, Albert

   Pieces (3), Op. 4
      Kistner (1887)

BELLON, J.

   Sonata, Op. 33 [orig: vln, pno]
      Costallat (Ney)

BELY, Viktor Aronovich (1904-)

   Poeme
      RussSt (1929)
      Universal

BENDA, Georg (1722-1795)

> *Concerto No. 1 in F*
> *Schott (Lebermann/May)
> *Sonata in E-flat* [vla, b.c.]
> Breitkopf (1762)

BENDIX, Hermann (1859- ?)

> *Nordische Romanze*
> Ms
> *Sonatas* (4)
> Ms

BEN-HAIM, Paul (1897-)

> *Songs without Words* (3)
> *IsMusPub

BENJAMIN, Arthur L. (1893-1960)

> *From San Domingo*
> Boosey (Primrose)
> *Jamaican Rumba*
> *Boosey (Primrose)
> *Sonata in e*
> Boosey (1947)
> *Sonata or Concerto, Elegy, Waltz,* and *Toccata* [orig: vla, orch]
> *Boosey
> *Le Tombeau de Ravel* (Valse caprices)
> *Boosey

BENNETT, David

> *Ballade*, Op. 16
> Oxford (Primrose)

BEREZOWSKY, Nicolai (1900-1953)

> *Concerto*, Op. 28 (1941)
> Boosey

BERGSMA, William (1921-)

Fantastic Variations on a Theme from Tristan
*Galaxy
Night Piece and Dance Piece (1942)
withdrawn

BERIOT, Charles Auguste de (1802-1870)

Serenade [orig: vln, pno]
*Belwin-Mills (Applebaum)

BERKELEY, Lennox (1903-)

Sonata in d
*Chester (1949)

BERKOWITZ, Sol

Introduction and Scherzo (Blues and Dance)
*Presser (1974)

BERLIOZ, Hector (1803-1869)

Harold in Italy, Op. 16 [orig: vla, orch]
Jobert (Liszt)

BERRY, Wallace T. (1928-)

Cantico lirico
*Fischer

BERTHOLD, Henry

Jewish Dances (5) (1963)
*DeutschVerMus

BESSEMS, Antoine (1809-1868)

La Flute enchantee de Mozart: Fantaisie
  Choudens (1860)
Souvenirs elegiaques, Op. 25
  Schott (1851)

BEYER, Frank Michael (1928-   )

Sonata [vla, org]
  *Bärenreiter

BEYTHIEN, Kurt (1897-   )

Sonata in D, Op. 13
  Hofmeister (1930)

BEZRUKOV, G.

Easy Pieces (3)
  *MezhdKniga

BIGOT, Eugène Victor (1888-   )

Theme and Variations
  *Durand

BILOIR, G.

Ballade, Cavatine, II. Gavotte
  Jobert (ca. 1910)

BINDER, Christlieb Siegmund (1723-1789)

Sonata in D [vlc ad lib]
  *Schott (Ruf)

BIZET, Georges (1838-1875)

Adagietto, from L'Arlésienne Suite [orig: orch]
  *Schott (Primrose)

Aria, from *L'Arlésienne Suite* [orig: orch]
  *Choudens
Intermezzo [vla, pno or vln, pno or vlc, pno]
  *Etling (Etling) (1971)

BLACHER, Boris (1903-)

Concerto, Op. 48
  *Bote&Bock

BLACKWOOD, Easley (1933-)

Sonata
  *Elkan-Vogel

BLANC, Adolphe (1828-1885)

La Farfalla, Scherzetto fantastique, Op. 7
  Costallat (ca. 1850)
Sonata in F, Op. 43 [orig: hn, pno]
  Costallat
Sonata No. 1 in G, Op. 12 [orig: vlc, pno]
  Costallat
Sonata No. 2 in c, Op. 13 [orig: vlc, pno]
  Costallat
Sonata No. 3 in C, Op. 17 [orig: vlc, pno]
  Costallat
Sonata No. 4 in g, Op. 47 [orig: vlc, pno]
  Costallat

BLENDINGER, Herbert

Chaconne [vla, org]
  *Orlando
Concerto
  *Orlando
Sonata [vla, hpscd]
  *Orlando

BLEUSE, Marc

    Alternative
      *Heugel (1974)

BLISS, Sir Arthur (1891-1975)

    Intermezzo, from *Piano Quartet* (1915)
      Oxford (Forbes)
    Sonata (1932)
      *Oxford (1934)

BLOCH, Ernest (1880-1959)

    Meditation and Processional
      *Schirmer
    Pieces (2) (1951)
      Schirmer
    Suite (1951)
      *Schirmer
    Suite Hébraique [orig: vla, orch]
      *Schirmer

BLOHM, Sven (1907-)

    Suite
      Svenska

BLOMFIELD-HOLT, Patricia (1910-)

    Suite No. 2 (1939) [vla, pno or vln, pno]
      *BMICan
      *Canadian (loan)

BLUMER, Theodor (1881-1964)

    Sonata, Op. 17
      Ms

BOCCHERINI, Luigi (1743-1805)

Concerto No. 3 in G [orig: vlc, orch]
  Schirmer
Sonata in c
  *Carisch (Sabatini)
  *Schott (Ewerhart)
Sonata No. 3 in g [orig: vlc, pno]
  *International (Alard/Meyer)
Sonata No. 6 in A [orig: vlc, pno]
  *International (Katims)

BOECK, Auguste de (1865-1937)

Fantasy
  Schott (ca. 1920)

BOHM, Carl

Perpetual Motion No. 6, from *Suite No. 3* [orig: vln, pno]
  *Fischer (Isaac/Lewis)

BOIS, Rob du (1934-)

Ut supra
  *Donemus (1973)

BOISDEFFRE, Charles-Henri-René de (1838-1906)

Berceuse, Op. 34
  Hamelle
Pieces (3), Op. 40
  *Hamelle (1873)

BONI, Pietro Giuseppe Gaetano

Largo and Allegro
  *MezhdKniga (Lepilov)

BONONCINI, Giovanni (1670-1747)

Rondeau in D
    Schott (Moffat) (1910)

BORNOFF, [?]

Fiddler's Holiday [vla or vla, pno]
    *Fischer
Violin Sings [vla or vla, pno]
    *Fischer

BORODIN, Aleksandr Porfir'evich (1833-1887)

Scherzo and Nocturne, from *String Quartet No. 2*
    Oxford (Primrose)

BORODKIN, [?]

Synco-Rhythmicon
    MusPubHold

BORRIS, Siegfried (1906-)

Canzona, Op. 110, No. 1 [vla, org or vla, hpscd]
    *Sirius
Kleine Suite
    *Sirius
Sonata in F, Op. 51
    *Sirius (1951)

BORTNIANSKY, Dimitri Stepanovitch (1752-1825)

Sonata in C
    Musgis

BORTOLOTTI, Mauro (1926-)

Combinazioni libere
    *Ricordi

BOSSI, Enrico (1861-1925)

Romance
Breitkopf

BOTTJE, Will Gay (1925-)

Fantasy Sonata
*AmCompAll

BOTTO VILLARINO, Carlos (1923-)

Fantasía, Op. 15 (1961-1962)
InstExtMus

BOURGES, Jean Maurice (1812-1881)

Sonata
pub by comp (ca. 1880)

BOURNONVILLE, Armand

Appassionato in c
*Billaudot
Costallat (1929)
Dance pour Katia
Costallat
Lamento
Costallat

BOWEN, Edwin York (1884-1961)

Melody for the G-String, Op. 47
Swan (1923)
Phantasie
Ms
Sonata No. 1 in c, Op. 18 (1907)
Schott (Tertis) (1907)

Sonata No. 2 in F, Op. 22 (1912)
Schott (1912)
Suite (1916)
Schott (1916)

BOYCE, William (1710-1779)

Tempo di Gavotta
Oxford

BOZZA, Eugène Joseph (1905-)

Concertino
Junne
*Ricard
Improvisation burlesque
*Leduc

BRAAL, Andries de (1909-)

Introduzione ed allegro cappriccioso
*Donemus

BRAEIN, Edvard Fliflet (1924-)

Serenade [orig: vla, orch]
*Lyche (1947)

BRAHMS, Johannes (1833-1897)

Germania (10 extracts)
*Heugel
Hungarian Dances Nos. 1 and *3* [orig: pno 4 hands]
*Hinrichsen (Forbes)
Sonata in e, Op. 38 [orig: vlc, pno]
*AmCompAll (Ferritto) (vla part only)
*International (Altmann)

Sonata in E-flat, Op. 120, No. 2 [vla, pno or clar, pno]
    *Augener
    *Breitkopf
    *International (Katims)
    Simrock
    *ViennaUrEd (Müller/Michaels/Seiler)
Sonata in F, Op. 99 [orig: vlc, pno]
    Simrock (Altmann)
Sonata in f, Op. 120, No. 1 [vla, pno or clar, pno]
    *Augener
    *Breitkopf
    *International (Katims)
    Patelson
    Schott
    Simrock
    *ViennaUrEd (Müller/Michaels/Seiler)
Sonata in G, Op. 78 [orig: vln, pno]
    Simrock (Klengel)
Sonata No. 2 in A, Op. 100 [orig: vln, pno]
    *Holly-Pix (Robin/Primrose)
Sonatas (2) in *f* and *E-flat*, Op. 120, Nos. 1 and 2 [vla, pno or clar, pno]
    *Henle
    *Peters
Sonatensatz: Scherzo in c, from the *F-A-E Sonata* [orig: vln, pno]
    *Doblinger (Stierhof)
    *International (Katims)
Waltz in A, Op. 39, No. 15 [orig: pno 4 hands]
    International (Borisovsky)
Waltz in E, Op. 39, No. 2 [orig: pno 4 hands]
    *Omega (Grunes)
Wie Melodien zieht es mir, Op. 105, No. 1 [orig: voice, pno]
    *Fischer (Primrose)
Wir wandelten, Op. 96, No. 2 [orig: voice, pno]
    Boosey (Tertis)

BRES, Jacques

    Air varie in C
        Costallat

BRESGEN, Cesar (1913-   )

Sonata No. 1 (1937-   )
Müller (1939)

BRÉVILLE, Pierre-Onfroy de (1861-1949)

Prière
Rouart
Sonata
*Eschig

BRIDGE, Frank (1897-1941)

Allegro appassionato
Stainer (1908)
Pensiero
Stainer (1908)

BRINGS, Allen

Sonata
*Seesaw

BRITTEN, Benjamin (1913-   )

Lachrymae (Reflections on a Song of Dowland), Op. 48
*Boosey (Primrose) (1951-1952)

BRIXI, František Xaver (1732-1771)

Concerto in C
*Schott (Lebermann)

BROMAN, Sten (1902-   )

Fantasy, Fugue and Chorale
Svenska

BROSSET, Jules

> *Pieces* (3)
> Leduc (1910)

BROVELLIO, H

> *Nocturne*
> Leduc

BROWN, James Clifford (1923-)

> *Air and English Jig*
> Stainer (1931)
> *Burletta*
> Stainer (1931)
> *Caprice*
> Salabert
> *Chauvre souris*
> Stainer
> *David of the White Rock*
> *Williams
> *Fling*
> Stainer
> *Pedlar*
> Stainer
> *Polychordia*, Set I, Nos. 1-6
> Stainer (1926)
> *Promenade*
> Stainer
> *Revellers*
> Stainer
> *Rondeau en musette*
> Stainer (1931)
> *Sprigged Muslin*
> Stainer
> *Tea-Time*
> Stainer
> *Viola d'Amore Waltz*
> Stainer

BROWN, Rayner (1912-)

Chorale Prelude on "Aus tiefer Not" [vla, org]
  *Western
Sonata [vla, org]
  *Western (1970)

BROWNE, P.

Snowy Breasted Pearl
  Williams

BROŽ, František (1896-1962)

Frühlingssonate, Op. 18 (1946)
  *Artia
  Statni

BRUCH, Max (1838-1920)

Kol Nidre, Op. 47 [orig: vlc, orch]
  *Fischer (Lehmann)
  *Peters (de Smet)
Romance in F, Op. 85 [orig: vla, orch]
  *Schott

BRUNEAU, Alfred (1857-1934)

Romance
  *Hamelle

BRUNNER, Hans (1898-)

Fantasy
  Ms
Sonatas (2), Op. 8 (1928) and Op. 26 (1942)
  Ms

BRUST, Herbert (1900-   )

   Bratschen-Musik in D, Op. 8
      VerDeutschTon (1920)

BRUSTAD, Bjarne (1895-   )

   Capricci
      Hansen

BRYARS, Gavin (1943-   )

   Long-Player
      *ExpMusCat

BUCHTEL, Forest L.

   Ambition Waltz
      *Kjos
   Happy Days
      *Kjos
   Jolly Fellows
      *Kjos

BUDDE, Kurt (1894-   )

   Sonatinas (1934)
      Ms

BÜSSER, Paul Henri (1872-1973)

   Appassionato
      Enoch
   Catalane
      Lemoine
   Rhapsodie arménienne, Op. 81 [orig: vla, orch]
      Costallat
      *Leduc

BULAKOV, P

Barcarolle
MezhdKniga

BUNIN, Revol Samuilovich (1924-)

Concerto, Op. 22
*MezhdKniga (Barshai)
Sonata, Op. 26
*MezhdKniga
*Peters (Barshai)

BURGMÜLLER, Friedrich (1806-1874)

Nocturnes (3)
*Augener (Hermann)

BURKHARD, Willy (1900-1955)

Concerto (1953)
*Bärenreiter

BURMESTER, Willy (1869-1933)

French Air [orig: vln, pno]
*Schott (Tertis)

BURTON, Eldin

Sonata
*Fischer

BUSH, Allan Dudley (1900-)

Dance Melody, from *Two Melodies*, Op. 47
Williams
Song Melody, from *Two Melodies*, Op. 47
*Williams

BUSONI, Ferruccio Benvenuto (1866-1924)

Albumblatt [vla, pno or vlc, pno]
Breitkopf (1917)

BUSTINI, Alessandro (1876-1970)

Sonata in g
Ricordi (1920)

BUTTERWORTH, David Neil (1934-)

French Pieces (2)
*Chappell

CAIX d'HERVELOIS, Louis de (ca. 1670-ca. 1760)

La Chambor: Allemande
*International (Marchet)
Melancholie d'amour
Benjamin
Suite No. 2 in D [orig: vl da gamba, hpscd]
Delrieu (Grabowska/Namer) (1952)

CAKRT, Miroslaw

Sonata
Ms

CALDARA, Antonio (1670-1736)

Canto
*Chester (Rostal)

CAMPAGNOLI, Bartolomeo (1751-1827)

Divertissements
Jobert (Ginot)
Theme and Variations, from *Caprices,* Op. 22
Moeck

CANTELOUBE DE MALARET, Marie-Joseph (1879-1957)

Bourrée auvergnate in A
Leduc

CAPDEVIELLE, Pierre (1906-1969)

Sonata
Ms

CAPITANO, Isidoro

Leggenda in a (1942)
Elkan-Vogel
Suvini-Zerboni

CAPOIANU, Dumitru (1929-   )

Sonata
Editura(Bucharest) (1955)

CARLES, Marc (1933-   )

Intensités
*Leduc

CARSE, Adam von Ahn (1878-1958)

Breezy Story
*Augener (1932)
Calm Reflections
Augener (1932)
Heartache
Augener
Thoughtfulness
Augener (1932)
Waltz Steps
*Augener

CARTER, Elliott Cook (1908-)

Elegy (1943) [vla, pno or vlc, pno]
*Peer-Southern
Pastoral (1940) [vla, pno or Eng hn, pno or clar, pno]
AmMusCen
*NewMus

CARTMILL, G. J.

Space Studies (2), Op. 9 (1937; rev. 1945)
NYPubLib

CASADESUS, Henri Gustave (1879-1957)

Morceau de concert
Mercier (1931)

CASIMIR-NEY, L.

Fantasie sur la sizilienne de A. Gouffle
Costallat (ca. 1850)

CASORTI, August

Divertissement, Op. 45
Leuckart (1867)
Piene de l'ame. Recit fantastique
Schweers (1887)

CAVALLINI, Eugenio (1806- ?)

Fantasie originali e variazioni
Ricordi
Souvenir and Polacca
Ricordi

CAZDEN, Norman (1914-)

Recitations (3), Op. 24a
Andrews

*pub by comp
Sonata, Op. 104a
*pub by comp

CECE, Alfredo (1902-   )

Recitativo [vla, pno or vln, pno]
    *Zanibon

CELLIER, Alexandro Eugène (1883-1968)

Sonata in G-flat
    Senart (1923)

CEREMUGA, Josef (1930-   )

Sonata elegica
    *Panton

CESARI, P.

Phantasie, on *Il Trovatore* of G. Verdi
    Ricordi (1862)

CEULEMANS, Ivo

Capriccio [vla, pno or vln, pno]
    *Schott(Brussels)
Sonatina
    Maurer (1962)

CHAĬKOVSKIĬ, Petr Il'ich (1840-1893)

Autumn Song, Op. 37a, No. 10 [orig: pno]
    *MezhdKniga (Borisovsky)
Aveux passionné [orig: pno]
    *MezhdKniga (Borisovsky)

Barcarolle ("June"), Op. 37a, No. 6 [orig: pno]
  *Chester (Forbes)
  SchmidtCF (Beda)
By the Fireside, Op. 37a, No. 1 [orig: pno]
  *MezhdKniga (Borisovsky)
Chanson triste (A Song of Sadness), Op. 40, No. 2 [orig: pno]
  *Fischer (Isaac/Lewis)
Chanson triste, Op. 40, No. 2; *Italienisches Liedchen*, Op. 39, No. 15
  [orig: pno]
  *Chester (Forbes)
Lullaby, from *Mazeppa* [orig: voice, orch]
  *MezhdKniga (Strakhov)
Melody, Op. 42, No. 3 [orig: vln, pno]
  *MezhdKniga (Strakhov)
Nocturne, Op. 19, No. 4 [orig: pno]
  *International (Borisovsky)
  RussSt (1940)
Nocturne, Op. 19, No. 4; *Snowdrop*, Op. 37a, No. 4 [orig: pno]
  *MezhdKniga (Borisovsky)
None but the Lonely Heart, Op. 6, No. 6 [orig: voice, pno]
  *Fischer (Hegner/Deery)
Song Without Words, Op. 2, No. 3 [orig: pno]
  *MezhdKniga (Strakhov)
Theme, from *Symphony No. 5*
  *Boston (Caruthers)
Valse sentimentale, Op. 51, No. 6 [orig: pno]
  *Omega (Grunes)
Variations on a Rococo Theme, Op. 33 [orig: vlc, orch]
  *Holly-Pix (Robin/Primrose)
White Nights, Op. 37, No. 5 [orig: pno]
  *MezhdKniga (Borisovsky)

CHAILLEY, Jacques (1910-)

Sonata
  *Leduc (1954)

CHALLAN, Henri (1910-)

Diptyque: 1. Andante
  *Leduc

Diptyque: 2. Rondo
  *Leduc

CHANDOSHKIN, Ivan. *See* Khandoshkin, Ivan Evstaf'evich

Chanson favorite d'Henri IV
  *Chester (Radmall)

CHAUSSON, Ernest (1855-1899)
  Interlude, from *Poeme de l'amour et de la mer*, Op. 19 (1889-1892)
    [orig: voice, orch]
    *International (Katims)
  Pièce, Op. 39
    Salabert

CHAYNES, Charles (1925-)
  Alternances
    *Leduc

CHEVILLARD, Paul Alexander Camille (1859-1923)
  Introduction and March, Op. 22
    Costallat (1905)
  Pieces (4), Op. 4 (1887)
    Enoch (1890)

CHILDS, Robert Barney (1926-)
  The Day Sequence: 1
    *AmCompAll

CHOISY, Frank Louis (1872-)
  Impressions d'Orient: Suite, Op. 135
    Leduc (1923)

CHOPIN, Fryderyk Franciszek (1810-1849)

Nocturne, Op. 9, No. 2 [orig: pno]
  *Fischer (Sarasate/Rehfeld)
Nocturne in c-sharp, Op. posth. [orig: pno]
  Schirmer (Vardi)

CHRISTOFF, Vincent [Crombruggen, Paul van] (1905-)

Kaleidophoon: Konzertstück
  Maurer (1962)

CIRRI, [Giovanni Battista] ([ca. 1740- ?])

Arioso
  Musicus

CLARKE, Henry Leland (1907-)

Nocturne
  *AmCompAll

CLARKE, Rebecca (1886-)

Passacaglia on an Old English Tune
  Schirmer (1943)
Pieces (2)
  Oxford (1930)
Sonata Atonal (1921)
  *Chester

CLEMENTI, Muzio (1752-1832)

Minuet [vla, pno or vln, pno or vlc, pno]
  *Etling (Etling) (1971)
Sonatina in C, Op. 36, No. 1 [orig: pno]
  *Belwin-Mills (Applebaum)

COATES, Gloria Kannenberg (1938-)

Fantasy on "How Lovely Shines the Morningstar" (1974) [vla, org]
Ms

COCCHIA, Fausto

Moto perpetuo
Forlivesi

COLAÇO OSORIO-SWAAB, Reine (1889-)

Sonata No. 3 (1952)
  *Donemus (1952)
Tsaddiék: Intermezzo
  *Donemus (1953)

COLLET, Henri (1885-1951)

Rapsodie Castillane, Op. 73 [orig: vla, orch]
Senart

COLLINGS, G.

Sonatina
Chester

COOKE, Arnold (1906-)

Sonata in F (1937)
Oxford (Cummings) (1940)

COOLEY, Carlton (1898-)

Concertino
  *ElkanH
Song and Dance
Senart

COOLS, Eugène (1877-1936)

Andante serio, Op. 98
　*Eschig (1923)
Berceuse, Op. 86
　*Eschig
Poème, Op. 74
　*Eschig

CORDERO, Roque (1917-　)

Tres mensajes breves
　*Peer-Southern

CORELLI, Arcangelo (1653-1713)

Adagio, from *Sonata in a*, Op. 5, No. 5　[orig: vln, b.c.]
　Peters (Klengel)
Allegro, from *Sonata in F*, Op. 5, No. 4　[orig: vln, b.c.]
　Peters (Klengel)
Prelude and Allemande
　*Belwin-Mills (Akon)
Sonata in a, Op. 5, No. 12 ("La Folia")　[orig: vln, b.c.]
　*International (David/Hermann)
　*Schott (Alard)
Sonata in d, Op. 5, No. 7　[orig: vln, b.c.]
　*International (Katims)
Sonata in F, Op. 5, No. ?　[orig: vln, b.c.]
　SAEM
Sonata da camera in G, Op. 4, No. 10　[orig: 2 vlns, b.c.]
　*Oxford (Forbes/Richardson) (1948)

CORTESE, Luigi (1899-　)

Improvviso, Op. 46
　*Curci

COSACCHI, Stephan

Berceuse, Op. 5d
　*Gerig

COSMA, Edgar (1925-   )

Sonatina
Editura(Bucharest) (1955)

COULTHARD, Jean (1908-   )

Sonata Rhapsody (1962)
*Canadian (loan)

COUPERIN, François (1668-1733)

Menuet, C. 292, and *Bourrée*, C. 414
Oxford (Forbes) (1948)
Suite, from *Concerts royaux* [orig: unspecified insts, b.c.]
Oxford (Forbes/Richardson) (1947)

COWELL, Henry (1897-1965)

Hymn and Fuguing Tune No. 7
*Peer-Southern (1953)

CRESTON, Paul (1906-   )

Homage, Op. 41 (1947) [vla, harp, org or vla, pno or str orch]
Schirmer (1959)
*Shawnee
Suite, Op. 13 (1937)
ProArt
Schirmer (1937)
*Templeton

CRUFT, Adrian (1921-   )

Impromptu in B-flat, Op. 22 [orig: pno]
MusUn
Williams

Romance, Op. 13
MusUn
Williams (1957)

CUI, César Antonovitch (1835-1918)
Orientale, from *Kaleidoscope*, Op. 50, No. 9 [orig: vln, pno]
*Fischer (Gottlieb/Saenger)

CUNDELL, Edric (1893-)
Rhapsody
Paxton (ca. 1920)

CUSTER, Arthur R. (1923-)
Parabolas
*General (1972)

CUTTER, Benjamin
Eine Liebesnovelle. 5 Bagatelles, Op. 20
SchmidtAP (1895)

DAHL, Ingolf (1912-1970)
Divertimento
Schott
*SPAM

DALE, Benjamin James (1885-1943)
Fantasy in D, Op. 4
Schott (1912)
Pieces
Ms
Romance, from *Suite in d*, Op. 2
Novello (1937)

Sonata
Ms
Suite in d, Op. 2 (1914)
Novello (Tertis)

DALLINGER, Fridolin
Sonata (1965)
*Doblinger

DAMROSCH, Leopold (1832-1885)
Liebegesang (Nocturne)
Schuberth (Ritter)

DANCLA, Jean Charles (1818-1907)
Theme and Variations [vla, pno or vln, pno or vlc, pno]
*Etling (Etling) (1971)

DARE, Marie
Le Lac
*Chester

DARGOMYZHSKIĬ, Aleksandr Sergeevich (1813-1869)
Elegy
*MezhdKniga (Borisovsky)

DAVID, Félicien César (1810-1876)
Concertino, Op. 12 [orig: bsn, pno]
*Billaudot
Costallat

DAVID, Gyula (1913-)
Concerto
*Budapest

DAVID, Johann Nepomuk (1895-)

Melancholia, Op. 53 (1958) [orig: vla, chamb orch]
*Breitkopf

DAVID, Thomas Christian (1925-)

Variations on a German Folk Song [vla, org]
*Doblinger

DAVIDOV, Karl IÙl'evich (1838-1889)

Romance [vla, pno or vln, pno or vlc, pno]
*Etling (Etling) (1971)
MezhdKniga

DAWE, Margery

Lonely Vale
*Cramer

DE BIASE, [?]

Reverie
*Fischer

DEBUSSY, Claude (1862-1918)

Beau soir [orig: voice, pno]
*International (Katims)
Clair de lune, from *Suite bergamasque* [orig: pno]
*Spratt (Cazden)
La Fille aux cheveux de lin, from *12 Préludes*, Book I [orig: pno]
RussSt (Borisovsky)
Il Pleure dans mon coeur, from *Ariettes oubliées* [orig: voice, pno]
Musicus (Hartmann)
Romance, from *Deux romances* (No. 1) [orig: voice, pno]
*International (Katims)

DECADT, Jean (1914-   )

Nocturne
*Metropolis

DECRUCK, F.

Sonata in c-sharp
*Billaudot

DE FESCH, Willem. *See* Fesch, Willem de

DEGEN, Helmuth (1911-   )

Sonata (1940)
Müller (1953)

DEHNERT, Max (1893-   )

Kleine Suite
Ms
Sonata
Ms

DE JONG, Marinus (1891-   )

Concerto, Op. 111
*Belgian

DELAUNAY, Rene (1880-   )

Fantaisie concertante (ca. 1920)
Ms

DELCROIX, Léon Charles (1880-1938)

Caprice, Op. 71
Buffet (1930)

DELDEN, Lex van (1919-   )

    Suite, Op. 4
        *Donemus (1949)

DELIUS, Frederick (1862-1934)

    Caprice and Elegy (1925) [orig: vlc, orch]
        Boosey
    Serenade, from *Hassan* [orig: orch]
        Boosey (Tertis)
    Sonata No. 2 [orig: vln, pno]
        *Boosey (Tertis)
    Sonata No. 3 [orig: vln, pno]
        *Boosey (Tertis)

DELMOTTE, Camille

    Concertino in c
        Maurer (1960)

DELVAUX, Albert (1913-   )

    Introduzione
        *Belgian

DESLANDES, F.

    Eclogue
        Enoch (1931)

DESSAU, Paul (1894-   )

    Sonatina
        Dresdner (1951)

DIABELLI, Anton (1781-1858)

    Sonatina in a
        *Hug (Baechi)

DI DONATO, Vincenzo (1887-1967)

Variations on a Theme of R. Schumann
   *Bongiovanni

DIETRICH, Oskar (1888-   )

Rondino
   Ms

d'INDY, Vincent. *See* **Indy, Vincent d'**

DINICU [?]

Hora staccato (Roumanian)
   *Fischer (Heifetz)

DITTERSDORF, Carl von. *See* **Ditters von Dittersdorf, Karl**

DITTERS VON DITTERSDORF, Karl (1739-1799)

Andantino
   *International (Primrose)
Concerto No. 3 in F, Krebs No. 168
   *Schott (Lebermann/Lutz)
Sonata in E-flat
   *Breitkopf (Schroeder)
   *Hofmeister (Mlynarczyk/Lürmann) (1929)
   *International (Vieland)

DOBIÁŠ, Vaclav (1909-   )

Balada
   Ms

DODGSON, Stephen (1924-   )

Francies (4)
   *Chappell

DOMAŽLICKÝ, František

Bagatelles (5)
*Panton

DOMINIK, Josef

Character Pieces (3), Op. 20
Hofmeister (1863)
Le Gondoliere: Cantilene, Op. 15
Hofmeister (1856)
Les Jouteurs: Scherzo, Op. 14
Hofmeister (1856)
Les Ondes: Impromptu, Op. 16
Hofmeister (1856)
Le Reve: Ballade, Op. 13
Hofmeister (1856)

DONATO, Anthony (1909-)

Sonnet (1945) [vla, pno or clar, pno]
AmCompAll

DONATO, Vincenzo di. *See* Di Donato, Vincenzo

DOPPELBAUER, Josef (1918-)

Concerto
*Doblinger

DOTZAUER, Justus Johann Friedrich (1783-1860)

Concertino in A, Op. 89
Simrock (1825)

DRAESEKE, Felix August Bernhard (1835-1913)

Sonata in c, Op. 56, No. 1 (1892)
Draeseke (1935)

Sonata in F, Op. 56, No. 2 (1901-1902)
Ms

DRESSEL, Erwin (1909-   )
  Partita
    *Ries&Erler
  Sonata, Op. 43
    Ms

DREYSCHOCK, Felix (1860-1906)
  Andante religioso, Op. 28
    Junne

DRIESSLER, Johannes (1921-   )
  Pieces (5), Op. 24, No. 3b
    *Bärenreiter (1953)

DRIGO, Riccardo (1846-1930)
  Serenade
    *Fischer (Schloming/Ambrosio)

DRUSCHETZKY, Georg (1745-1819)
  Concerto in D
    *SimBenjRaht (Schwamberger)

DUBLANC, Emilio A. (1911-   )
  Sonata, Op. 6 (1942)
    UnivNacCuyo (1946)

DUBOIS, Théodore (1837-1924)
  Andante cantabile
    Heugel (ca. 1890)

Suite de danses [orig: vla, orch]
*Leduc

DUBOVSKÝ, Milan

Sonatina
*Slovenský

DUHAMEL, M.

Chats de la fiancée (2)
Rouart (ca. 1920)
Soniou an dous
Rouart (ca. 1920)

DUKE, John Woods (1899-)

Melody in E-flat
*Elkan-Vogel

DUNHILL, Thomas Frederick (1877-1946)

Pieces (4)
Williams (1928)

DUVERNOY, Victor-Alphonse (1842-1907)

Lied, Op. 47
Hamelle (1906)

DVARIONAS, Balys (1904-)

Theme and Variations
*MezhdKniga (Lepilov)

DVOŘÁK, Antonín (1841-1904)

Bagatelle, Op. 47, No. 3 [vla, pno or vln, pno; orig: 2 vlns, vlc, harmonium]
*Hinrichsen (Forbes)

Concerto in b, Op. 194 [orig: vlc, orch]
   *International

DYDO, Stephen

   Fantasy and Variations
      *AmCompAll

DYER, John

   In Cheerful Mood
      *Williams
   Mantilla in e
      Augener (1950)
   Meditation
      *Augener
   Woodland Serenade in D
      Augener (1950)

DYSON, Sir George (1883-1964)

   Prelude, Fantasy and Chaconne [orig: vla, orch]
      *Novello

EBEL VON SOSEN, Otto (1899-   )

   Arioso im alten Stil
      Litolff (1958)

ECCLES, Henry (fl. 1694-1735)

   Prelude and Courante, from *Sonata in g* [vla, pno or vln, pno or vlc, pno;
      orig: vln, hpscd]
      *Etling (Isaac) (1971)
   Sonata in g [orig: vln, hpscd]
      *International (Katims)
      *Peters (Klengel)

EDELSON, Edward

Night Song
Musicus

EDER, Helmut (1916-)

Sonatina, Op. 34, No. 2
*Doblinger

EDMUNDS, Christopher M. (1899-)

Pieces (4)
*Lengnick
Sonata in D
*Novello (1956)
Windmill
*Lengnick

EFFINGER, Cecil (1914-)

Melody
*Presser

EISEL, Günther (1901-)

Sonata in c-sharp (ca. 1950)
Ms

EISMA, Will (1929-)

Sonatina
*Donemus (1971)

EISNER, C.

Pièces de salon (2), Op. 16 [orig: vla, orch]
Hofmeister (1863)

ELGAR, Sir Edward William (1857-1934)

Canto popolare
  Novello
Concerto in e, Op. 85 [orig: vlc, orch]
  *Novello (Tertis)
Theme from *Pomp and Circumstance*, Op. 39 [orig: orch]
  *Fischer (Akers)
Very Easy Pieces (6), Op. 22 [orig: vln]
  *Bosworth

ELÍAS, Manuel Jorge de (1939-)

Preludio (Pieza de cámera Núm. 1) (1962)
  Ms

ENESCO, Georges (1881-1955)

Concertpiece in F (1908)
  Enoch
  *International

ENRIQUEZ, Manuel (1926-)

Piezas (4)
  Ms

ERMOLOV, Alexis
Concertino russe, Op. 31
  pub by comp (ca. 1919)
Valse-fantaisie
  pub by comp

ERNST, Heinrich Wilhelm (1814-1865)

Élégie, Op. 10 [orig: vln, pno]
  Schuberth

ERSFELD, Christian

Ständchen, Op. 10 [orig: vln, str orch]
Simon

ETLER, Alvin Derald (1913-)

Sonata [vla, hpscd]
*Continuo

EVANS, David Emlyn (1843-1913)

Moto perpetuo
Williams (1938)

EVETT, Robert (1922-)

Sonata (1958)
*AmCompAll

FÄRBER, Otto (1902-)

Suite, Op. 58
Maurer (1959)

FAHNE, [?]

Divertissement, Op. 23
Brandenburg (1844)

FARJEON, Harry (1878-1948)

Morceaux (2) (1912)
Schott

FARKAS, Ferenc (1905-)

All'Antica
*Budapest

Arioso
  *Budapest
  Kultura
  Zenemükiado
Roumanian Folk Dances
  *Budapest
  Kultura
  Zenemükiado
Sonata (1927)
  Zenemükiado

FARNABY, Richard (ca. 1560-1640)

Nobodye's Gigge–Bonny Sweet
  *Chester (Radmall)

FASCH, Johann Friedrich (1688-1758)

Sonata in A [vla, hpscd]
  Breitkopf (1762)
Sonata in C
  *McGinnis (Doktor) (1965)

FAURÉ, Gabriel Urbain (1845-1924)

Après un rêve (After a Dream), from *3 Songs*, Op. 7 [orig: voice, pno]
  *International (Katims)
Elegy, Op. 24 [orig: vlc, orch]
  *International (Katims)
Lamento
  *International (Katims)
Piece
  *Leduc
Sicilienne, Op. 78 [orig: vlc, pno]
  *International (Katims)

FAYE-JOZIN, Fred de

Konzertstück
  Rouhier (1932)

FEBRE, W.
   Sonata (1930)
      Ms

FELD, Jindřich (1925-)
   Sonata
      *Panton

FELDERHOF, Jan (1907-)
   Aria
      *Donemus (1974)

FELDMAN, Morton (1926-)
   The Viola in My Life 3
      *Universal

FELDMANN, Z.
   Jüdische Gesänge (2) (1932)
      Ms

FERGUSON, Howard (1908-)
   Irish Folk-Tunes (5)
      Oxford (Forbes) (1928)
   Short Pieces (4), Op. 6
      *Boosey (1937)

FERIR, Emile
   Le Menetrier: Mazurka
      Schott (1911)
   Serenade
      Schott (1925)

FESCH, Willem de (1687-1757?)

Sonatas, Book I (6) [vla, b.c.; orig: vln, b.c.]
  *Bärenreiter (Woehl)
Sonatas, Book II (6) [vla, b.c.; orig: vln, b.c.]
  *Bärenreiter (Woehl)

FIBICH, Zdeněk (1850-1900)

Poem [orig: pno]
  *Fischer (Ambrosio/Isaac/Lewis)
Sonatina in d, Op. 27
  Urbanek

FICHER, Jacobo (1896-   )

Pieces (3), Op. 76 (1953)
  Ms
Sonata, Op. 80 (1953)
  Ms

FIÉVET, Paul (1892-   )

Sonata, Op. 10 [orig: vlc, pno]
  Buffet

FILA, C.

Fancy Fiddlin'
  *Concert (Muller)
Happy Strings
  *Concert

FINCH, Ronald

Romanza
  *Chester

FINKE, Fidelio F. (1891-)
Sonata
   *Breitkopf (1955)

FINNEY, Ross Lee (1906-)
Sonata in a
   *Peters
Sonata No. 1 (1937)
   Ms
Sonata No. 2 (1953)
   *Henmar (Courte) (1971)

FIORILLO, Dante (1905-)
Sonata (1929)
   Ms

FIRKET, Leon (1839- ?)
Concert Piece in d
   Schott (1878)
Romance
   Comptoire

FITELBERG, Jerzy (1903-)
Serenade in F [vla, pno or vln, pno]
   *Peer-Southern (1954)

FLACKTON, William (1709-1793)
Sonata in C, Op. 2, No. 1 [No. 4] (1770) [vlc ad lib; orig: vla, b.c.]
   *Doblinger (Sabatini) (1960)
   *Lengnick (Cullen) (1955)
   *Schott (Bergmann)
Sonata in D, Op. 2, No. 2 (1770) [vlc ad lib; orig: vla, b.c.]
   *Doblinger (Sabatini) (1960)

Sonata in G, Op. 2, No. 3 [No. 6] (1770) [vlc ad lib; orig: vla, b.c.]
   *Doblinger (Sabatini) (1960)
   *Schott (Bergmann)
Sonata in C, Op. 2, No. 8 [orig: vla, b.c.]
   *Schott (Bergmann)

FLEMING, Robert (1921-)

   Berceuse [vla, pno or vln, pno or vlc, pno]
      *Canadian (loan)

FLEURY, H.

   Fantasy, Op. 18
      Enoch (ca. 1910)

FLOSSMAN, Oldrich (1925-)

   Jesenická Suita
      *Artia

FOCK, A.

   Berceuse
      Eschig (ca. 1925)

FOCK, Gerard von Brucken (1859-1935)

   Sonata in b, Op. 5
      Breitkopf (1889)

FORST, Rudolf (1900-1973)

   Homage to Ravel
      Benjamin
      Musicus

FORSYTH, Cecil (1870-1941)

Chanson celtique
Schott
Concerto in g
*Schott (Ireland)

FORTINO, Mario

Prelude and Rondo
Tritone

FORTNER, Wolfgang (1907-)

Concertino in g (1934) [orig: vla, orch]
Schott

FOSS, Hubert James (1899-)

Three Airs for Two Players
Oxford

FOSTER, Stephen Collins (1826-1864)

Jeanie with the Light Brown Hair [orig: voice, pno]
*Fischer (Heifetz/Primrose)

FOX, K. Dorothy (1934-)

Sonata
Senart (1930)

FRANCK, César Auguste (1822-1890)

Sonata in A [orig: vln, pno]
*International (Vieland)

FRANCK, Maurice (1897-   )

Suite
*Transatlantiques
Theme and Variations [orig: vla, orch]
*Durand

FRANCOEUR, François (1698-1787)

Sonata No. 4 in E
*International (Alard/Dessauer)

FRANKEN, Wim (1922-   )

Sonata (1953; rev. 1972) [vla, pno or clar, pno]
*Donemus (1972)

FRANKLIN, Howard

Moonlight on the River
Fischer

FREED, Isadore (1900-1960)

Rhapsody [orig: vla, orch]
*Fischer

FRESCOBALDI, Girolamo Alessandro (1583-1643)

Toccata [orig: org]
Moeck

FREY, Emil (1889-1946)

Pieces (3), Op. 79 (1936)
Ms

FRICKER, Peter Racine (1920-)

  Concerto, Op. 20
     *Schott

FRID, Géza (1904-)

  Sonatina, Op. 25 (1946)
     *Donemus (1949)

FRID, Grigory S.

  Concerto
     *MezhdKniga

FRISKIN, James (1886-1967)

  Elegy
     Stainer (1915)

FRÖHLEN, Max (1901-)

  Sonata in E-flat, Op. 8
     *Bote&Bock
     Hiob (1948)

FUCHS, Lillian

  Caprices (12) [orig: vla]
     *Boosey

FUCHS, Robert (1847-1927)

  Fantasy Pieces (6), Op. 117
     Robitscheck (1927)
  Sonata in D, Op. 86
     Robitscheck (1909)
     *Wollenweber

FÜRST, Paul Walter (1926-   )

Sonata, Op. 33
  *Doblinger (1962)
Sonatina, Op. 13 (1952)
  *Doblinger

FULEIHAN, Anis (1900-1970)

Recitative and Sicilienne [vla, pno or vlc, pno]
  *Peer-Southern (1945)
  Schirmer

FULTON, Robert Norman (1909-   )

Introduction, Air and Reel
  Oxford
Sonata da camera
  *Chester

GABRIEL, Wolfgang (1930-   )

Sonata
  Ms

GADZHIBEKOV, Uzeir (1885-1948)

Azerbaijan Folk Song
  MezhdKniga

GÄHRICH, Wenzel (1794-   ?)

Concertino in B-flat, Op. 2
  Breitkopf (1831)

GAÏGEROVA, Varvara Adrianovna (1903-1944)

Suite
  *MezhdKniga

GÁL, Hans (1890-)
Sonata, Op. 101
  *SimBenjRaht (1973)
Suite, Op. 102a
  *SimBenjRaht (1973)

GALUPPI, Baldassare (1706-1785)
Aria amorosa
  Augener (Tertis)

GANTSCHER, Alexis
Sonata
  Ms

GARAEW, G.
Pieces (5)
  GosMusIzd (1952)

GARCIN, Jules (1830- ?)
Concertino, Op. 19 [orig: vla, orch]
  Lemoine

GARD, Jules
Fantasy
  Costallat (ca. 1850)

GARDNER, Samuel (1891-)
From the Canebrake, Op. 5, No. 1 [orig: vln, pno]
  *Schirmer (1958)

GARLICK, Antony

A Piece for Any Occasion
*Seesaw

GAUBERT, Philippe (1879-1941)

Ballade
*Eschig

GAWROŃSKI, Wojciech Adalbert (1868-1910)

Sonata, Op. 22
Moeck
*PolWydMuz (Szaleski)

GEIER, Oskar (1889-   )

Sonata, Op. 6 (1926)
Ms

GEIFMANN, A.

Poeme (1933)
Ms
Poeme-Rhapsodie (1934)
Ms
Sonata (1936)
Ms

GEISLER, Johann Christian (1729-1815)

Sonata in d, Op. 10
*Skandinavisk

GEISSLER, Fritz (1921-   )

Sonata
*Peters

Sonatina
    *Breitkopf (1954)

GENISCHTA, J. (1795- ?)
    Klassische Sonate in drei Sätzen
        RussVer
    Sonata, Op. 19
        RussSt (1961)

GENZMER, Harald (1909-)
    Sonata in D
        *Ries&Erler (1940)
    Sonata No. 2
        *Bärenreiter (1958)
    Sonatina
        *Litolff (1973)
        *Peters

GERHARD, Fritz Christian (1911-)
    Concerto (1954)
        *Möseler

GERHARD, Roberto (1896-1970)
    Sonata (1950)
        Ms

GERMANO, Carlo (1830-)
    Fantaisie sur Faust de Gounod, Op. 7
        Ricordi (ca. 1870)

GERSTER, Ottmar (1897-)
    Concertino, Op. 16 [orig: vla, orch]
        Schott (1930)

Concerto
  Schott
Sonata
  Hofmeister (1955)
Sonata in d
  *Hofmeister (1956)

GESSINGER, Julius (1899-)
  Festliche Romanze
  Ms

GHEBART, Joseph (1796- ?)
  Concert No. 1, Op. 55
  Costallat

GHENT, Emmanuel (1925-)
  Entelechy
  *Oxford

GIAMPIERI, Alamiro (1893-1963)
  Fantasia
  *Ricordi (1939)

GIARDA, Luigi Stefano (1868-1953)
  Kleine Stücke (3), Op. 24 [orig: vlc, pno]
  Rahter (1899)
  Lied ohne Wörte, Op. 31 [orig: vlc, pno]
  Ricordi

GIDEON, Miriam (1906-)
  Sonata
  *AmCompAll

GIFFORD, Alexander

Aria
Augener (1935)
Irische Wiesen: 12 Folktunes
Schott (1952)
Madrigal and Meditation
Augener (1927)
Song of the River Lark
Augener (1927)

GILTAY, Berend (1910-)

Miniatures (4)
*Donemus

GIORDANI, Tommaso (ca. 1733-1806)

Madrigal
RussSt (Borisovsky) (1936)
Sonata in B-flat [orig: vla, b.c.]
*Schott (Ruf)

GIORNI, Aurelio

Sonata [orig: vlc, pno]
Schirmer

GIPPS, Ruth (1921-1965)

Lyric Fantasy, Op. 46
*Fox

GIRNATIS, Walter (1894-)

Sonata piccola
Ms

GIVOTOWSKI, T.

Konzertstück in d (ca. 1930)
Ms

GLASER, Werner Wolf (1910-)
Capriccio No. 2
Ms

GLAZUNOV, Aleksandr Konstantinovich (1865-1936)
Elegy in g, Op. 44 [orig: vla, orch]
*Belaieff
GosMusIzd
*International
Grezy, Op. 24 [orig: hn, pno]
Belaieff
GosMusIzd
Serenade espagnole, Op. 70
Belaieff
GosMusIzd
Jobert (Ginot)

GLIÈRE, Reinhold Moritsevich (1875-1956)
Prelude; Romance; Rondo
*MezhdKniga

GLINKA, Mikhail Ivanovich (1804-1857)
Barcarolle [orig: pno]
*MezhdKniga (Borisovsky)
Children's Polka [orig: pno]
*MezhdKniga (Borisovsky)
Mazurka [orig: pno]
*MezhdKniga (Borisovsky)
Pieces (3)
MezhdKniga

Sonata
    *McGinnis
Sonata in d (1825-1828)
    *MusRara (Borisovsky) (1961)
    Universal

GLUCK, Christoph Willibald, Ritter von (1714-1787)

Andante cantabile
    Schott (Moffat)
O del mio dolce ardor
    Benjamin
    *ElkanH (Elkan)
Pieces (4)
    MezhdKniga

GODARD, Benjamin Louis Paul (1849-1895)

Berceuse, from *Jocelyn*
    *Fischer (Isaac/Lewis)

GOEB, Roger (1914-)

Concertant III C
    *AmCompAll

GOEDICKE, Alexander Fedorovitch (1877-1957)

Prelude
    MezhdKniga

GOEMKE, A.

Preludes (24), Op. 59
    RussSt (1954)

GÖPFERT, Karl A. (1768- ?)

Sonata facile in E-flat, Op. 35 [orig: hn, pno]
    Hofmeister (1923)

GÖRING, Ludwig

Impromptu and Romance
   Hofmeister (1882)
Pieces (3), Op. 4
   Kahnt (1884)

GOLESTAN, Stan (1875-1956)

Arioso and Allegro de concert [orig: vla, orch]
   Salabert (1933)

GOLTERMANN, Georg Eduard (1824-1898)

Andante (Cantilena from Concerto in a, Op. 14) [orig: vlc, orch]
   *Fischer (Roth/Isaac/Lewis)
Ballade, Op. 41, No. 2
   Schott
Duos, Op. 15 and 25 [orig: vlc, pno]
   Peters
Grand Duo, Op. 15 [orig: vlc, pno]
   Augener (Such)
Sonatina in A, Op. 36
   Peters
Sonatina in G, Op. 61
   André
Sonatina in F, Op. 114 [orig: vlc, pno]
   Augener (Kreutz)

GOLUBEV, Evgeniĭ Kirillovich (1910-)

Concerto, Op. 47
   *MezhdKniga

GOSSEC, François Joseph (1734-1829)

Gavotte
   *Fischer (Isaac/Lewis)

GOTTWALD, Heinrich (1821- ?)

L'Amitie: Romance, Op. 26
Oertel (1898)

GOULD, Morton (1913-)

Concerto
*Belwin-Mills

GOUVY, Louis Théodore (1819-1898)

Serenade venitienne
Schott (1875)

GOW, David Godfrey (1924-)

Nocturne and Capriccio, Op. 31
*Augener (Forbes) (1957)

GRABNER, Hermann (1886-)

Pieces (2), Op. 4
Schuberth (1908)
Sonata in g: Hausmusik, Op. 47, No. 4
*Kistner (1943)

GRAENICHER, Ernst

Sonata
Ms

GRANADOS Y CAMPIÑA, Enrique (1867-1916)

Danza española No. 2: Oriental [orig: pno]
*International (Katims)
*UnMusEsp (Amaz)

Danza española No. 5: Andaluza [orig: pno]
*UnMusEsp (Amaz)
Danza española No. 6: Rondella Aragonesa [orig: pno]
*UnMusEsp (Amaz)

GRATTANN, W. H.

Sehnsucht: Impromptu, Op. 35 [orig: vln, pno]
Hart (1874)

GRÁUE, C. D.

Menuetto scherzando, Op. 27
Kistner

GRAUN, Johann Gottlieb (1699?-1771)

Sonata in c [W. F. Bach?]
Sikorski (1962)
Sonata No. 1 in B-flat [vlc ad lib; orig: vln, b.c.]
*Breitkopf (Wolff)
Sonata No. 2 in F [vlc ad lib; orig: vln, b.c.]
*Breitkopf (Wolff)

GRAUN, Karl Heinrich (1704-1759)

Allegro in B-flat
Peters (Meyer)

GRAVEL, [?]

Solo No. 1 [vla, b.c.]
Breitkopf (1767)

GRAZIOLI, Giovanni Battista (ca. 1750-ca. 1820)

Sonata in F
*Galliard (Marchet)

GREEN, Ray (1909-)
Concertante
AmMusEd

GREENE, Maurice (1696-1755)
Allemanda, from *A favourite lesson for the harpsichord* [orig: hpscd]
Oxford (Forbes) (1952)

GREGH, Louis (1843-1915)
Chat du Bûcheron [orig: pno]
Rouart

GREIVE, G.
Melody, Op. 4
Costallat (1851)
Hofmeister

GRENZ, Arthur (1909-)
Fantasy, Op. 12
*Sikorski (1953)

GRIBOLEDOV, A
Waltzes
Ms (Borisovsky)

GRIEG, Edvard Hagerup (1843-1907)
Erotikon, from *Lyriske Stykker*, Book III, Op. 43, No. 5 [vla, pno or
vln, pno or vlc, pno; orig: pno]
*Etling (Etling) (1971)
Sonata in a, Op. 36 [orig: vlc, pno]
*International
*Peters (Platz)

Sonata in G, Op. 13 [orig: vln, pno]
  Breitkopf (Dessauer)
To the Spring, from *Lyriske Stykker*, Book III, Op. 47, No. 6 [orig: pno]
  *Oxford (Forbes)

GRIMM, Friedrich-Karl (1902-   )

Nordische Erzählungen, Op. 54, No. 1 and Op. 55, No. 2
  VerMKW (1936)
Sonata (1931)
  Ms

GROSS, Paul (1898-   )

Concerto
  Ms

GROSSMAN, Ferdinand (1887-1970)

Cantilena
  *Concert

GROVLEZ, Gabriel Marie (1879-1944)

Romance, Scherzo, and Finale
  *Heugel (1932)

GRUDZIŃSKI, Gzwsław (1911-   )

Miniatures
  Polnischer (1957)
  *PolWydMuz (Gonet)

GRÜTZMACHER, Friedrich Wilhelm (1832-1903)

Romance, Op. 19b
  Kahnt

GUARNIERI, Mozart Camargo (1907-)
Sonata (1950)
Ms

GUÉNIN, Marie Alexandre (1744-1835)
Concerto No. 1 in D, Op. 14
Sieber

GUERRINI, Guido (1890-1965)
Arcadica [orig: ob, pno]
Curci
Aria di ciociaria
Bongiovanni

GURLITT, Cornelius (1820-1901)
Buds and Blossoms, Op. 107, No. 4
Augener (Kreutz)

GUTCHE, Gene (1907-)
Interlude, Op. 25 (1950)
AmCompAll

HAAKMAN, J. Jacques
Character Pieces (3), Op. 8 [orig: vln, pno]
Woolhouse (1899)
In Distant Lands. 3 Pieces, Op. 22 [orig: vln, pno]
Schirmer (1898)
Mélodies Faciles (10), Op. 26 [orig: vln, pno]
Schott (1900)

HABERSACK, Karl (1904-)
Sonata, Op. 61
Ms

Theme with Variations and Fugue, Op. 62, No. 3
Ms

HÄRTEL, A.

Evening Serenade
    *Fischer (Tobani)
    Kistner (1892)
    Seeling (1902)

HÄSSLER, Johann Wilhelm

Élégie
    RussSt (Borisovsky)

HAHN, Reynaldo (1875-1947)

Soliloque et forlane
    Eschig

HAIDMAYER, Karl

Sonata No. 1 (1964)
    *Bärenreiter (1971)

HÁJEK, Aleš

Sonata No. 2
    *Panton

HALBERSTADT, Josef

Elegy
    Schott (1875)

HALLNÄS, Johan Hilding (1903-)

Legende
    Svenska

Sonata, Op. 19
  Nordiska

HALM, August

Grande sonate in F, Op. 25 [orig: vlc, pno]
  Diabelli (1847)

HAMANN, Erich (1898-)

Sonata, Op. 33
  *Doblinger (1952)

HAMBLEN, Bernard (1877-)

Reverie
  *Boosey

HAMBURG, Gregor (1900-)

Aus dem hohen Lied, Op. 5, Nos. 1 and 2
  Universal (1928-1929)

HAMILTON, Iain Ellis (1922-)

Sonata, Op. 9 (1950-1951)
  *Schott (1954)

HAMMER, Franz Xaver (ca. 1750-1813)

Sonata No. 2 in D
  Musicus
  Peters (Meyer)
Sonata No. 3 in G
  Peters (Meyer)
Sonata No. 4 in G
  Peters (Meyer)

HANDEL, George Frideric (1685-1759)

Air in F [orig: hpscd]
  Schott (Moffat)
Album of 7 Easy Pieces
  *Bosworth (Borowski)
Andante in a
  Novello (Ritter)
Andante, from *Sonata in b*, Op. 1, No. 9 [orig: fl, b.c.]
  Peters (Klengel)
Arietta
  *Schott (Tertis)
Arrival of the Queen of Sheba
  *Oxford (Forbes)
Concerto [compilation]
  *Oxford (Barbirolli/Primrose)
Concerto in b [compilation]
  *Eschig (Casadesus)
  RussSt (Casadesus) (1935)
  Schott (Casadesus)
Concerto in g
  Schuberth (Schröder)
Largo
  Augener
Minuet, from *3 Lessons for the Harpsichord* [orig: hpscd]
  Peters (Klengel)
Prelude in D [orig: hpscd]
  Oxford (Forbes) (1948)
Preludium [orig: hpscd]
  *Shapiro (Sontag)
Sonata in a [vla, hpscd]
  Breitkopf (1762)
Sonata in C vla, hpscd or vl da gamba, hpscd; orig: vl da gamba, hpscd]
  *Augener (Jensen)
  *Bärenreiter (Längin)
  *International (Jensen)
  *Schott (Hoffmann)
Sonata in g [orig: vl da gamba, b.c.]
  *International (Katims)

Sonata in e, Op. 1, No. 2 [orig: fl, b.c.]
*ElkanH (Courte)
Sonata in A, Op. 1, No. 3 [orig: vln, b.c.]
*International (Hermann/Vieland)
Sonata in a, Op. 1, No. 4 [orig: treble rec, b.c.]
*Ricordi (D'Ambrosio)
Sonata in G, Op. 1, No. 5 [orig: fl, b.c.]
Oxford (Forbes)
Sonatas (2) *in a*, Op. 1, No. 4, and *G*, Op. 1, No. 5 [orig: treble rec,
b.c. (No. 4), fl, b.c. (No. 5)]
Williams (Shore)
Sonata in g, Op. 1, No. 10 [orig: vln, b.c.]
*International (Alard/Meyer)
*Schott (Dart)
Sonata in A, Op. 1, No. 14 [orig: vln, b.c.]
*Oxford (Forbes/Richardson)
Sonata in E, Op. 1, No. 15 [orig: vln, b.c.]
*Williams
Three Movements, from *Water Music Suite* [orig: orch]
*Shapiro (Sontag)

HANDOSHKIN, Ivan. *See* **Khandoshkin, Ivan Evstaf'evich**

HANESYAN, Harutyun

Andantino
*Eschig
Prelude and Capriccio
*Eschig
Romance
*Eschig

HANUŠ, Jan (1915-)

Sonatina, Op. 37
*Artia (1956)

HARDEBECK, C. G.

The Lark in the Clear Air
Augener

HARRIS, Roy (1898-   )

Soliloquy and Dance (1938)
Oxford (1938)
Schirmer (1941)

HARRIS, Russell G.

Variations
*AmCompAll

HARRISON, Julius Allan (1885-1963)

Sonata in c
*Lengnick (1946)

HARRISON, Pamela (1915-   )

Lament
Galliard

HARSÁNYI, Tibor (1898-1954)

Sonata
*Heugel (1958)

HARTLEY, Walter Sinclair (1927-   )

Sonata
*Fema

HARTMANN, Karl Amadeus (1886-   )

Concerto
*Schott

HASENÖHRL, Franz (1885-)

Sonata (1928)
Ms

HASSE, Johann Adolph (1699-1783)

Bourrée and Minuet
MezhdKniga
Dances (2)
Schott (Moffat)

HAUBIEL, Charles (1892-)

Lullaby
*Seesaw

HAUFRECHT, Herbert (1909-)

Caprice
*Bourne

HAUG, Hans (1900-1967)

Fantasia concertante [orig: vla, orch]
*Curci

HAUSE, Karl

Abschieds-Fantasie
Oertel (ca. 1880)

HAUSER, Miska (1822-1887)

Berceuse (Cradle Song)
*Fischer (Ambrosio/Isaac/Lewis)
Gavotte, Op. 56
Schuberth (Dessauer)

HAY, Frederick Charles (1888-1945)

Concerto in a, Op. 16
Tischer (1928)

HAYDN, Franz Joseph (1732-1809)

Adagio, from *String Quartet in f*, Op. 20, No. 5 [vla, pno or vln, pno]
Oxford (Forbes) (1953)
Air
Augener
Andante
Oxford (Forbes) (1948)
Capriccio
Schott (Burmester/Tertis)
Concerto in D, Hob. VIIb/2 [orig: vlc, orch]
*Breitkopf (Gevaert)
*International (Spitzner)
Divertimento
*Elkan-Vogel (Piatigorsky/Elkan)

HAYDN, Michael (1737-1806)

Concerto in C, Perger No. 55 [orig: vla, org, str orch]
*Doblinger (Angerer)

HEIDEN, Bernhard (1910-   )

Sonata (1959)
*Associated

HEINZE, Berthold (1870-   )

Andante and Capriccio
Ms

HELM, Everett Burton (1913-   )

Sonata (1944)
Ms

HEMEL, Oscar van (1892-)

Sonata (1942)

*Heuwekemeijer (1946)

HENNEBERG, Carl Albert Theodor (1901-)

Serenata
Nordiska

HENNESSY, Swan (1866- ?)

Sonata celtique, Op. 62
*Eschig (1925)

HENSS, Heinrich

Lied ohne Worte, Op. 2 [orig: vln, pno]
Bosworth (1914)

HERMANN, E.

Notturno rimesso, Op. 27
*Augener

HERMANN, Friedrich (1828-1907)

Andante, Scherzo, Romance, Mazurka, Op. 1
Peters (1855)
Easy Exercises and Pieces (12)
*Augener
Pieces (6), Op. 15
Rieter (1878)

HERMANN, Karl (1876-)

Pieces (2), Op. 6
Zimmermann (1923)

Variationen über eine ernste Weise (6)
  Zimmermann (1923)

HERNÁNDEZ-LÓPEZ, Rhazes (1918-   )
  Sonata (1952)
  Ms

HERTEL, [?]
  Solo No. 1 [vla, b.c.]
  Breitkopf (1767)

HERZOGENBERG, Heinrich von (1843-1900)
  Legends (3), Op. 62
  Peters (1918)

HESS, Carl
  Sonata in b, Op. 6 [orig: vlc, pno]
  Kistner (1879)

HILL, Alfred Francis (1870-1960)
  Concerto
  *Peer-Southern (1969)

HILL, Wilhelm (1838-   ?)
  Notturno, Scherzo, Romance, Op. 18
  André (1869)
  Romances (2), Op. 22
  Gebauer (1869)

HINDEMITH, Paul (1895-1963)
  Concerto, Op. 48 (1930)
  *Schott (Willms)

Kammermusik No. 5: Concerto, Op 36, No. 4 (1927)
  *Schott (Willms)
Meditation, from *Nobilissima visione* (1938) [orig: orch]
  *Schott (1938)
Der Schwanendreher (1935) [orig: vla, chamb orch]
  *Schott (Hindemith)
Sonata in F, Op. 11, No. 4 (1922)
  *Schott (1950)
Sonata in C (1939)
  *Schott (1940)
Trauermusik (1936) [orig: vla, str orch]
  *Schott (Willms)

HIPMANN, Silvester (1893-)

  Weihnachtselegie (1939)
  Ms

HIVELY, Wells (1902-1969)

  Psalmody
  *AmCompAll

HODDINOTT, Alun (1929-)

  Concertino [orig: vla, chamb orch]
  *Oxford

HÖFFER, Paul (1895-1949)

  Viola Music (1946)
  *Mitteldeutscher

HÖLLER, Karl (1907-)

  Sonata in E, Op. 62
  *Schott

HOFFMEISTER, Franz Anton (1754-1812)

Concerto in D
 *Eschig (Vieux)
 *Grahl
 *International (Doktor)

HOFFSTETTER, Romanus (1742-1815)

Concerto in C
 *Schott (Lebermann/May)
Concerto No. 1 in E-flat
 *Süddeutscher (Gottron)

HOFMANN, Heinrich Karl Johann (1842-1902)

Reverie in C, Op. 45
 Brockhaus (1878)

HOFMANN, Richard (1844- ?)

Sonatina in F, Op. 46
 Kistner (1885)

HOLBROOKE, Joseph Charles (1878-1958)

Romance in D, Op. 59
 Ms

HOLLAND, Theodore Samuel (1878-1947)

Ellingham Marshes
 *Hinrichsen
Suite in D (1935)
 Boosey (1938)

HOLST, Gustav Theodore (1874-1934)

Lyric Movement [orig: vla, chamb orch]
 *Oxford (I. Holst) (1971)

HOLST, Imogen Clare (1907-)

Easy Pieces (4)
*Augener (1935)

HONEGGER, Arthur (1892-1955)

Sonata (1920)
*Eschig

HONNORÉ, Leon

Morceau de concert [orig: vla, orch]
DuWast (1890)
*Gilles

HOOK, James (1746-1827)

Sonatina
*Belwin-Mills (Applebaum)

HOVHANESS, Alan (1911-)

Talin, Concerto, Op. 93
*Associated

HOWARD, John Tasker (1890-1964)

Still Waters
Musicus

HOYER, Karl (1891-)

Sonata in A, Op. 30 (1923)
Simrock (1923)

HRISANIDE, Alexandru Dumitru (1936-)

Sonata (*Music*) (1965)
*Gerig

HRUŠKA, Jaromir Ludvik (1910-   )
Sonata
   *Artia

HUBAY, Jenő (1858-1937)
Morceau de concert, Op. 20 [orig: vlc, orch]
   Hainauer (1893)

HÜBSCHMANN, Werner (1901-   )
Concerto (1928)
   Ms

HÜE, Georges Adolphe (1858-1949)
Thème varié [orig: vla, orch]
   *Heugel

HUHN, Ernst Joachim (1894-   )
Sonatina, Op. 50
   pub by comp (1941)

HUMMEL, Bertold (1925-   )
Sonatina
   *Simrock

HUMMEL, Johann Nepomuk (1778-1837)
Fantaisie [orig: vla, str orch]
   *Transatlantiques
Sonata in E-flat, Op. 5, No. 3
   André (ca. 1798)
   *Doblinger (Doktor) (1960)
   *McGinnis (Rood)
   *Schott (Lebermann)

HUMPERDINCK, Engelbert (1854-1921)

Evening Prayer, from *Hansel and Gretel* [orig: voice, orch]
  *Boston (Caruthers)

HUNDT, Aline

Traumesgestalten, Zwei Tonstücke, Op. 6
  Simrock (1865)

HUNKE, Joseph (1801- ?)
  Elegy
    Bessel (1882)

HURÉ, Jean (1877-1930)
  Petite chanson
    Salabert

HURLSTONE, William Yeates (1876-1906)
  Characteristic Pieces (4) [vla, pno or clar, pno]
    Novello

HURNÍK, Ilja (1922-)
  Sonata, Op. 26
    *Artia (1956)
    Statni (1956)

HUSA, Karel (1921-)
  Poem (1959) [orig: vla, chamb orch]
    *Schott

HUSS, Henry Holden (1862-1953)
  Sonata in d, Op. 34 (1915)
    Ms

Sonata (1922)
    Ms

IBERT, Jacques (1890-1962)
    Aria
      *Leduc

ILYINSKY, Alexander Alexandrovitch (1859-1919)
    Berceuse
      *Chester (Forbes)

INDY, Vincent d' (1851-1931)
    Lied, Op. 19 [orig: vlc, orch]
      *International
    Sonata in D, Op. 84 (1924-1925)
      Rouart (1926)

INGHELBRECHT, Désiré Émile (1880-1965)
    Impromptu
      *Leduc (1922)
    Nocturne
      Salabert
    Prelude and Saltarello
      Eschig
      Mathot (1905)
      Salabert

IPPOLITOV-IVANOV, Mikhail Mikhailovich (1859-1935)
    Piece [orig: pno]
      MezhdKniga

IPUCHE-RIVA, Pedro (1924-   )
    Sonata en re (1959-1961)
      Ms

IRELAND, John (1879-1962)
Sonata
  *Augener (Tertis)

ISHII, Kan (1921-)
Sonata
  *Ongaku

IŠTVÁN, Miloslav (1928-)
Ronda
  *Artia

IVANOV-BORETZKY, Mikhail Vladimirovitch (1874-1936)
Sonata (1930)
  Musgis
  RussSt (1947)

IVÁNOV-RADKÉVICH, Nikolai Pavlovich (1904-1962)
Sonata (1926)
  Musgis
Sonata-Poem
  *MezhdKniga

IWANOW-RADKOWITSCH, D.
Sonata (1930)
  Ms

JACOB, Gordon Percival Septimus (1895-)
Air and Dance
  *Oxford
Concerto (1925)
  Oxford (1926)

Pieces (3)
    Curwen
    Novello
Sonatine (1948) [vla, pno or clar, pno]
    *Novello

JACOBI, Frederick (1891-1952)

Fantasy
    *Fischer

JACOBI, Wolfgang (1894-)

Sonata
    *Sikorski (1956)

JACOBSON, Maurice (1896-)

Berceuse (1946); *Lament* (1941); *Salcey Lawn* (1948)
    Oxford (1948)
Humoreske (1948)
    *Lengnick
Salcey Lawn
    Augener (1946)

JACOBY, Hanoch (1909-)

Concertino [orig: vla, orch]
    *IsMusPub
King David's Lyre
    *IsMusPub

JACQUES-DALCROZE, Émile (1865-1950)

Chant melancolique et romance, Op. 2
    Rouart (1892)

JÄRNEFELT, Armas (1869-1958)

Berceuse
  *Fischer (Deery)

JAHN, Raimund (1924-)

Sonata in E-flat, Op. 15 (1952)
  Ms

JANSA, Leopold (1795-1875)

Cantilene, Op. 84
  Schott (1867)

JEREMIÁŠ, Jaroslav (1889-1919)

Sonata, Op. 3
  Artia (Hyska)
  Statni (Hyska)

JEREMIÁŠ, Otakar (1892-)

Sonata, Op. 3
  *Artia

JERVIS-READ, Harold Vincent (1883-1945)

Melody in G
  Augener (1909)

JESINGHAUS, Walter (1902-1966)

Sonata, Op. 36 (1935)
  Ms
Sonatina brevis, Op. 22a
  Carisch (1939)

JIRÁK, Karel Boleslav (1891-)

   Sonata in C, Op. 26
     Simrock (1926)

JOACHIM, Joseph (1831-1907)

   Hebräische Melodien, Op. 9
     Augener (1883)
     Breitkopf (1888)
   Variations on an Original Theme, Op. 10
     Augener
     Breitkopf (1855)

JOACHIM, Otto (1910-)

   Music (1953)
     Ms

JOKISCH, Reinhold (1848- ?)

   Lyric Pieces (3), Op. 4
     Kistner (1891)

JOLAS, Betsy (1926-)

   Points d'aube [orig: vla, 13 winds]
     *Heugel (1973)

JONES, Daniel Jenkin (1912-)

   Pieces (8) (1948)
     Ms
   Sonata (1937)
     Ms

JONGEN, Joseph (1873-1953)

   Allegro appassionato, Op. 68 (1931) [orig: pno trio]
     *Leduc (1931)

Concertino, Op. 111 (1940)
Eschig
Introduction and Dance, Op. 102 (1935)
Eschig
Suite (1929) [orig: vla, orch]
*Lemoine
Suite en deux parties, Op. 48 (1915) [orig: vla, orch]
Lemoine

JONGEN, Léon (1884-   )
Pastorale and Gigue
*Brogneaux

JONSSON, Josef Petrus (1887-1969)
Fantasia elegiaca
Svenska

JORA, Mihail (1891-1971)
Sonata, Op. 32
Ms

JOSTEN, Werner (1885-1963)
Sonata
Associated (1938)

JOUBERT, John (1927-   )
Sonata, Op. 6
*Novello (1954)

JULLIEN, René (1878-   )
Concertstück in c, Op. 19 [orig: vla, orch]
Simrock (1912)

Lied, Op. 36
    *Eschig

JUNGMANN, Louis (1832- ?)

Intermezzo, Op. 9
    Hofmeister (1862)

JUON, Paul (1872-1940)

Sonata in D, Op. 15
    *International (Katims)
    *Lienau
Sonata in F, Op. 82 [vla, pno or clar, pno]
    Schlesinger

JURDZIŃSKI, Kazimierz (1894-1960)

Sonata
    *PolWydMuz

KABALEVSKIĬ, Dmitriĭ Borisovich (1904-)

Improvisation, Op. 21, No. 1
    *MCA (Kievman)
Prelude [orig: pno]
    RussSt (1954)

KABALIN, Fedor

Poem and Rhymes
    Triton

KADLEC, A.

Souvenir de Ch. Davidoff, Op. 31 [orig: vlc, pno]
    Jurgenson (1892)

KADOSA, Pál (1903-)

Concertino, Op. 27 [orig: vla, orch]
*Budapest

KALAŠ, Julius (1902-)

Concerto in d, Op. 69
*Artia

KAĽKBRENNER, Friedrich Wilhelm Michael (1785-1849)

Duos, Op. 11
Sieber
Grand Duo in d, Op. 63 [orig: fl, pno]
Simrock

KALL, Frederic

Pieces (4)
Boosey (1933)

KALLIWODA, Johann Wenzel (1801-1866)

Nocturnes (6), Op. 186
*International
*Peters

KALLSTENIUS, Edvin (1881-1967)

Visa ur "Dalarapsodi" [vla, org or vlc, org]
*Eriks

KAPR, Jan (1914-)

Fantasy (1937)
Hudebni (1942)

KARG-ELERT, Siegfried (1877-1933)

Sonata No. 2 in B-flat, Op. 139b
  *Zimmermann

KARKOFF, Maurice Ingvar (1927-   )

Liten Romans (1959)
  Svenska

KAUFFMANN, Leo Justinus (1901-   )

Kleine Suite
  Schott (1939)

KAUFMANN, Armin (1902-   )

Sonatina, Op. 53, No. 2
  *Doblinger

KAY, Ulysses Simpson (1917-   )

Sonata (in one movement) (1939)
  Ms

KEGEL, Karl (1770-   ?)

Eine Sommernacht: Nocturne, Op. 78 [orig: vla, chamb orch]
  Bellmann (1881)

KELDORFER, Robert (1901-   )

Sonata (1964)
  *Doblinger

KELLER, Homer (ca. 1917-   )

Sonata
  *AmCompAll

KELLEY, Robert (1916-   )

   Sonata (1950)
      *AmCompAll

KELTERBORN, Rudolf (1931-   )

   Moments (9) (1973)
      *Bote&Bock

KELZ, Johann Friedrich (1786-   ?)

   Variations on "Mein Schatz ist ein Reiter," Op. 210
      Junne (1840)

KEMPE, Harald (1900-   )

   Sonatina (1952)
      Svenska

KENINS, Talivaldis (1919-   )

   Partita breve (1971)
      *Canadian (loan)

KERSTERS, Willem (1929-   )

   Sonata, Op. 6
      Maurer (1962)

KESNAR, Maurits (1900-1957)

   Armenians
      Gamble
   Evening Campfire
      Gamble
   Halloween
      Gamble

In Memoriam
Gamble
Menuet antique
Gamble
Puppet Dance
Gamble
Shadow Picture
Gamble

KETÈLBEY, Albert William (1875-1959)

In a Monastery Garden
*Warner (MacLean)

KHANDOSHKIN, Ivan Evstaf'evich (1747-1804)

Concerto in C
*International (Vieland)
*MezhdKniga
*Peters (Jampolski)

KHATCHATURIAN, Aram (1903-   )

Suite
Ms

KIEL, Friedrich (1821-1885)

Romances (3), Op. 69
*Amadeus (1972)
Bote&Bock (1877)
*Eulenburg
*MusRara (1972)
Sonata in g, Op. 67
*Amadeus (1972)
Bote&Bock
*Eulenburg
*Wollenweber

KIEPERT, Max

> *Romance*, Op. 22
> *Heinrichshofen

KIESGEN, A.

> *Concertino*
> Hamelle

KIRCHBACH, Max

> *Traumbild* [orig: vln, pno]
> Hug (1901)

KIRCHNER, Theodor (1823-1903)

> *Pieces* (8), Op. 79
> Hofmeister

KIRKOR, Georgiĭ Vasil'evich (1910-)

> *Concert Fantasy*, Op. 26
> *MezhdKniga
> *Pieces* (2), Op. 18
> Musgis (1953)

KITTLER, Richard (1924-)

> *Sonatina* (1959)
> *Doblinger

KJELDAAS, Arnljot (1916-)

> *Sonata in g*
> Norsk

KLASS, Julius (1888-   )
  Sonata, Op. 40
    *Heinrichshofen
  Sonata in B-flat, Op. 36 (1932)
    Ms
  Tondichtungen (6)
    Heinrichshofen (1940)

KLEEMAN, Hans (1883-   )
  Suite (ca. 1925)
    Ms

KLENNER, John
  Fantasia [orig: vla, orch]
    Sprague

KLINGLER, Karl (1879-   )
  Sonata in d
    Simrock (1909)

KOCH, Sigurd Christian Erland von (1910-   )
  Larghetto [vla, pno or vlc, pno]
    *Peer-Southern
  Lyric Episode (1944)
    Ms
  Scherzo [vla, pno or vlc, pno]
    *Peer-Southern

KOCHER-KLEIN, Hilda
  Reigen, from *Suite in D*, Op. 16
    Klett (1925)
  Suite in D, Op. 19 (1925)
    Ms

KOCIPINSKI, Anton

> *Tesknota*, Op. 11
> Ms

KODÁLY, Zoltán (1882-1967)

> *Adagio in C* (1905; rev. 1916) [vla, pno or vln, pno or vlc, pno]
> *Budapest
> Zenemükiado

KOECHLIN, Charles Louis Eugene (1867-1950)

> *Sonata*, Op. 53
> Senart (1923)

KÖHLER, Moritz (1855- ?)

> *Elegy*, Op. 31
> Jurgenson (1899)

KÖLL, F.

> *Concinien* (4) (1966) [vla, pno or vlc, pno]
> *Breitkopf

KÖLLE, Konrad (1882-)

> *Concerto in A*, Op. 38
> Hofmeister (1931)

KOETSIER, Jan (1911-)

> *Concertino*
> *Peters

KOHOUTEK, Ctirad (1929-)

> *Suita*
> Ms

KOMPANEETZ, Zinovi (1902-   )

Poem-Monologue
   *MezhdKniga

KONING, Servaas de (?   -ca. 1720)

Sonata in d (ca. 1700)
   Broekmans (1948)

KOPPRASCH, Wilhelm

Introduction with Variations [orig: vla, orch]
   Ms

KORÍNEK, Miloslav

Komorné Koncertino
   *Slovenský
Sonatína
   *Slovenský

KORINGER, Franz

Sonata (1949)
   Ms
Sonatina
   *Doblinger

KORNAUTH, Egon (1891-1959)

Pieces (3), Op. 47
   *Doblinger (1955)
Sonata in c-sharp, Op. 3 (1913)
   Doblinger (1913)
   Universal
Sonatina, Op. 46a
   *Doblinger

KOSSENKO, Viktor (1896-1938)

Sonata
   Ms

KOTSCHETOFF, W.

Melody, Op. 5
   RussSt

KOUGUELL, A.

Suite dans le style ancien
   Gallet (Vieux) (1951)

KOVACS, [?]

Happy Days
   Fischer

KOZLOVSKY, Alexei (1905-   )

Sonata
   *MezhdKniga

KRANCHER, Willy

Rhapsody
   *Metropolis

KRATOCHWIL, Heinz (1933-   )

Sonata (1961)
   *Doblinger

KREIN, Alexander Abramovich (1883-1951)

Prologue in F, Op. 2
   RussSt
   Universal (1930)

KREJČÍ, Miroslav (1891-1964)

Compositions (3), Op. 34b (1932)
   Ms
Sonata in c-sharp, Op. 57
   *Artia (Hyska) (1944)
   Hudebni

KŘENEK, Ernst (1900-   )

Sonata (1948)
   Affiliated (1953)

KREUZ, Emil (1867-   ?)

Concerto in C, Op. 20
   Augener
Frühlingsgedanken; 3 Pieces, Op. 9
   Augener
Liebesbilder; 3 Pieces, Op. 5
   Augener (1890)
Pensée fugitive, Op. 13, No. 4
   ElkanH
Prelude and Melody
   Augener (1895)
Sonata in a, Op. 13, No. 6
   Augener
   Schott (1911)
Suite of Pieces, Op. 45
   Augener (1897)
The Violist. A Series of Progressive Pieces, Op. 13
   Book I. *12 Very Easy Pieces*
   Book II. *Progressive and Easy Pieces*
   Book III. *Progressive Melodies*
   Book IV. *Progressive Melodies*
   Book V. *Three Easy Sketches*
   Book VI. *Sonata in a*
      *Augener

KRIST, Joachim

Gleich un gleich
    *Orlando

KROGH, Theodor von

Sonatina (1952)
    Ms

KROL, Bernhard (1920-   )

Konzertante Musik, Op. 6 [orig: woodwind octet]
    *Breitkopf
Lassus Variations, Op. 33 [vla, hpscd or vla, pno]
    *SimBenjRaht

KRUG, Gustav (1803-   ?)

Adagio and Rondo, Op. 4
    Schuberth (1845)

KRUIKOV, Vladimir Nikilaievitch (1902-1960)

Nocturne
    Musgis (1930, 1959)
Novelle
    Musgis (1930, 1959)
Pavane
    Musgis (1959)
Pieces (2), Op. 13
    GosMusIzd (1950)
    *MezhdKniga
Pieces (4), Op. 18
    Ms
Reverie, Op. 8 (1920)
    Ms
Sonata in F, Op. 115 (ca. 1930)
    RussSt (1959)

KUBIZEK, Augustin (1918-   )

Sonatina, Op. 5a   [vla, pno or vlc, pno or clar, pno]
*Doblinger

KUDELSKI, Karl Matthias (1805-   ?)

Concertstück in e, Op. 127bis   [orig: vlc, pno]
   Schuberth (1869)
Fantasy, Op. 10
   Schuberth (1860)

KÜCKEN, Friedrich Wilhelm (1810-1882)

Sonata in D, Op. 12, No. 1   [orig: vlc, pno]
   Augener (1882)
Sonata in a, Op. 13, No. 1   [orig: vlc, pno]
   Augener (1882)
Sonata in C, Op. 13, No. 2   [orig: vlc, pno]
   Augener (1882)
Sonata in E-flat, Op. 16, No. 2   [orig: vlc, pno]
   Augener (1882)

KUFFERATH, Louis (1811-1882)

Réponse à l'élégie de H. W. Ernst   [orig: vln, pno]
   Schott (Kreuz) (1890)

KUHN, Siegfried (1893-   )

Sonata in b, Op. 7
   *Peters (Matz)
   Ries&Erler (1927)

KUHNEL, Paul

Concertino in G, Op. 2   [orig: vln, pno]
   André (1903)

KUKUCK, Felicitas

   Aus tiefer Not. 1. Partita [vla, org or vla, pno]
     *Hänssler
   Fantasia
     *Möseler

KUMMER, Hans (1880-)

   Pieces (2), Op. 9 [orig: Eng hn, pno]
     VerMKW (1926)

KUNC, Pierre

   Sonata in b
     Buffet (1924)

KUPKA, Karel (1927-)

   Tři dialogy
     *Panton (r)

KURTÁG, György (1926-)

   Concerto
     *Budapest

LABEY, Marcel (1875-1968)

   Sonata in C (1905)
     Eschig

LABITZKY, Joseph (1802-1881)

   L'Adieu. Romance sans paroles, Op. 286
     Schott (1872)

LABROCA, Mario (1896-   )
Suite (1923)
*Suvini-Zerboni (1950)

LACERDA, Osvaldo (1927-   )
Sonata (1962)
Ms

LACH, Robert (1874-1958)
Sonata in e, Op. 25
Günther (1932)

LACOMBE, Paul (1837-1927)
Morceau de fantaisie, Op. 133
Hamelle (1909)

LACROIX, Eugène (1858-   ?)
Premières tendresses
Costallat

LALO, Édouard Victor Antoine (1823-1892)
Chants russes, from Concerto russe, Op. 29 (1883) [orig: vln, orch]
    Hamelle (Neuberth)
Concerto in d (1876) [orig: vlc, orch]
    Bote&Bock (Casadesus) (1901)
    *International (Casadesus)
Sonata [orig: vlc, pno]
    *Heugel (Casadesus)

LAMOTE DE GRIGNON, J.
Canco de Maria [orig: vln, pno]
*UnMusEsp (Amaz)

Rêverie ("Schumanniana") (1901) [orig: vln, pno]
  *UnMusEsp (Amaz)

LANDAU, Victor
  Scherzo
  *AmCompAll

LANGER, Hans Klaus (1903-)
  Theme and Variations
  Astoria (1958)

LANGEY, Otto (1851-1922)
  Gavotte, Op. 43 [orig: vln, pno]
  Oertel (1898)

LAPARRA, Raoul (1876-1943)
  La Corde de l'automne, from *Le Jouer de violé*
  Heugel (1933)
  Suite ancienne en marge, from *Don Quichotte* [orig: vla, orch]
  Heugel

LAPON, Ed.
  Romance
  Durand

LARSSON, Lars Erik Vilner (1908-)
  Concertino No. 9, Op. 45 [orig: vla, str orch]
  *Boosey

LAUB, Ferdinand (1832-1875)
  Morceaux (3), Op. 14
  Jurgenson (1883)

LAUBACH, Alfred

Scottish Songs (20)
Augener (1888)

LAURENS, Edmond (1852- ?)

La Sièste
Fromont (1885)

LAURISCHKUS, Max (1876-1929)

Miniatures, Op. 4 [orig: clar, pno]
Simon

LAVÍN, Carlos (1883-1962)

Dos Versículos budistas (1936)
Ms

LE BEAU, Louise Adolpha (1850- ?)

Pieces (3), Op. 26
Kahnt (1883)

LECLAIR, Jean Marie (1697-1764)

Sarabande in C [orig: vln, b.c.]
Schott
Sarabande and Tambourin [orig: vln, b.c.]
Ries&Erler
Schott(London)
Sonata in c, "Le Tombeau" [orig: vln, b.c.]
*International (David/Hermann)
Sonata in D, Op. 9, No. 3 [orig: vln, b.c.]
Schott (Dessauer/Piatti)

LEDENEV, Roman Semenovich (1930-)

Concerto-Poem, Op. 13
*MezhdKniga

LEE, Louis (1819-1896)

Sonata in C, Op. 9 [orig: vlc, pno]
Schuberth (1861)

LEE, Sebastian (1805-1887)

Pièces mélodiques (7) [orig: vlc solo]
Schott (Krall)

LEGLEY, Victor (1915-)

Elegiac Lied, Op. 70
*Belgian
Sonata, Op. 13 (1943)
*Belgian
Spring Poem, Op. 51, No. 2
*Belgian

LEICHTENTRITT, Hugo (1874-1951)

Sonata, Op. 13 (ca. 1910)
pub by comp

LEIGHTON, Kenneth (1929-)

Fantasia on the Name Bach
*Novello (1957)

LEITERMEYER, Fritz

Episodes (12), Op. 36
*Doblinger

LENNARD, M.

Romance in F [orig: vln, pno]
Stöppler

LEONCAVALLO, Ruggiero (1858-1919)

Serenade [orig: vla, str orch]
Brockhaus (Hermann)

LESSLE, Adolf

Capriccioso [orig: vln, pno]
Baltischer (1926)

LETELIER-LLONA, Alfonso (1912-)

Sonata (1949)
InstExtMus

LETZTE, Rose

Irisches Volkslied
Seeling

LEVITCH, Leon (1927-)

Sonata, Op. 11 (1957)
Ms

LEVY, Frank (1930-)

Sonata ricercare (1972)
*Seesaw

LEWIN, Zara

Poème
RussSt (1930)
Universal

LEY, Salvador (1907-)
Piece (1956)
Ms

LIADOV, Anatolii Konstantinovich (1855-1914)
Prelude, Op. 11, No. 1 [orig: pno]
*MezhdKniga (Borisovsky)

LIATOSHYNS'KYI, Borys Mykolaïvych (1895-)
Pieces (2), Op. 65
Mistetstwo (1964)

LIDHOLM, Ingvar (1921-1964)
Invention
Svenska

LIEHNER, H
Sonatina [vla, pno or vln, pno or vlc, pno]
*Etling (Etling) (1971)

LIGH, Walter
Sonatina
Ms

LILIEN, Ignace (1897-1964)
Musica (1950)
*Donemus (1951)

LIMBERT, Frank (1866-1938)
Sonata in C, Op. 7
Hofmeister (1892)

LINK, Emil

Chant d'amour. Mélodie romantique [orig: vla, str orch]
SchmidtCF (1897)

LISZT, Franz (1811-1886)

Consolations (1849-1850) [orig: pno]
*Augener (Hermann)
Breitkopf
Notturno. Liebestraum No. 3 [orig: pno]
Ms (Borisovsky)
Romance oubiliée (1880) [vla, pno or vln, pno or vlc, pno]
Benjamin
*Budapest
*Sirorski
Sonetto 104 and *123 di Petrarca* [orig: pno]
Ms (Borisovsky)

LLOYD, Charles Harford (1849-1919)

Suite in the Old Style [orig: clar, pno]
Hawkes (1914)

LOBLOV, Bela

Rococo [vla, pno or vln, pno]
Blake

LOCATELLI, Pietro Antonio (1695-1764)

Sonata in g [orig: vln, b.c.]
*International (David/Hermann)
Sonata in g, Op. 6, No. 12 [orig: vln, b.c.]
*International (Doktor)

LOEB, David

Sonata No. 1
*Branch

LOEILLET, Jean Baptiste (1680-1730)

    Sonata in B-flat [orig: fl, b.c.]
        *International
    Sonata in f-sharp [orig: fl, b.c.]
        *International

LOHSE, Fred (1908-)

    Sonata
        *Metropolis (1960)

LOLIVREL, L.

    Sérénade de printemps
        *Eschig

LOLLI, Antonio (ca. 1730-1802)

    Sonata [orig: vln, keyboard]
        Lemoine (1920)

LONDON, Edwin (1929-)

    Sonatina
        *NewValley

LONGO, Alessandro (1864-1945)

    Suite in D, Op. 53
        Ricordi (1911)
    Tempo di Gavotta (3), Op. 22 [orig: vln, pno]
        Breitkopf (Hermann)

LONQUE, Georges (1900-)

    Concertos Nos. 1, and *2 in d,* Op. 15 ("Romantique")
        Bode-Vinck (1931)

Images d'orient, Op. 20 (1935) [orig: vla, orch]
    Leduc

LÓPEZ BUCHARDO, Carlos (1881-1948)
    Pieces (2)
        Ricordi (Bandini) (1928)

LORENZITI, Bernard (1764- ?)
    Sonatas (3), Op. 9
        Bojer (1810)
    Sonatas (3), Op. 39
        David (ca. 1828)

LOTTI, Alessandro
    Arie pur dicesti
        Urbánek (Moravec) (1935)

LOVELL, Joan Isabell
    Country Sketches (4)
        *Augener
    Easy Tunes (44)
        *Oxford

LUCERNA, Eduard
    Sonata (1939)
        Ms

LÜBECK, Louis (1838-1904)
    Albumblatt, Op. 19, No. 1 [orig: vlc, pno]
        Steingräber (1904)
    Träumerei, Op. 20 [orig: vlc, pno]
        Challier (Koenecke) (1905)

LUENING, Otto (1900-)

Suite [vla, pno or vlc, pno]
*Highgate (1972)

LÜTHGE, H.

Am Springbrunnen
MüllerF (1919)

LULLY, Jean Baptiste (1632-1687)

Arioso and Gavotte, from *Atys*
Ms (Borisovsky)
Gavotte in D and *Musette in d*
Schott (Moffat) (1910)
Gavotte and Rondeau, from *Alceste*
Augener (Stehling)
Schott

LUMBYE, Hans Christian

Traumbilder [orig: orch]
Breitkopf (1900)

LUNDÉN, Lennart Suneson (1914-1966)

Suite
Nordiska

LUTYENS, Elisabeth Agnes (1906-)

Concerto
Lengnick
Sonata, Op. 5, No. 4
*Belwin-Mills

LUTZ, Oswald (1908-)

Sonata
Ms

LUŽEVIČ, Franjo (1903-)

Pei Satiričnih Anekdot (Five Satirical Anecdotes)
    *Društva

MAASZ, Gerhard (1906-)

Music
    *Bärenreiter (1949)

McBRIDE, Robert Guyn (1911-)

Workout
    Associated

MacDOWELL, Edward Alexander (1861-1908)

To a Wild Rose, from *Woodland Sketches*, Op. 51, No. 1 [orig: pno]
    *Belwin-Mills (Applebaum)
    *Fischer (Isaac)

McEWEN, Sir John Blackwood (1868-1949)

Pieces
    Ms
Sonata in a
    Ms
Sonata No. 2 in f (1913) [orig: vln, pno]
    Anglo-French (1915)
    Oxford

McKAY, George Frederick (1899-)

Tlingit (Suite on Alaskan Indian Songs and Dances)
    *McGinnis

MACONCHY, Elizabeth (1907-)

Sonata (1938)
    Ms

MACZEWSKY, Amadeus

Pieces (6), Op. 3
Breitkopf

MAES, Jef (1905-)

Andante rustique
Maurer
Concerto
*Belgian
Intermezzo
Maurer

MAGANINI, Quinto (1897-)

Concert Album
Musicus (1954)
Night Piece
Musicus (Forst) (1946)
Song of a Chinese Fisherman
Musicus (1944)

MAGDIĆ, Josip (1937-)

Satirical Anecdotes (5)
*Društva

MAIBEN, William (1953-)

Pieces (4) (1971)
Ms

MAILLY, Alphonse-Jean-Ernest (1833-1918)

Causerie
Schott (Ritter) (1900)

MAJOCCHI, L.

Divertimento (Variations)
Ricordi (ca. 1850)

MAJORELLE, P.

Sonata
*Billaudot

MAKAROV, Evgenyi Petrovich (1912-   )

Sonata, Op. 5
*MezhdKniga

MAKAROVA, Nina Vladimirovna (1908-   )

Andantino
Ms (Borisovsky)

MAKOVSKY, Ludwig

Sonata in c
Ms

MALIGE, Fred (1895-   )

Concerto
*Breitkopf

MALIPIERO, Gian Francesco (1882-1973)

Canto nell'infinito
Leduc (1954)

MANN, Leslie D. (1924-   )

Sonata, Op. 17 (1962)
*Canadian (loan)

MANNINO, Franco (1924-)

Piccola sonata
  *Sonzogno

MANNS, Otto

A Northern Cradle Song, Op. 11
  Novello (1904)

MANSURIAN, Tigran

Sonata
  *MezhdKniga

MARAIS, Marin (1656-1728)

Fantasy
  *Leduc (R. Boulay/L. Boulay)
Old French Dances (5)
  *Chester (Aldis/Rowe)
Sarabande
  Durand (van Waefelghem)
Suite in D
  *Peters (Dalton)

MARCELLO, Benedetto (1686-1739)

Sonata in F [orig: vlc, b.c.]
  Patelson (Vardi)
Sonata in e, Op. 2, No. 2 [orig: vlc, b.c.]
  Augener (1906)
  *Galliard (Marchet)
  *International
Sonata in g, Op. 2, No. 4 [orig: vlc, b.c.]
  *Ricordi (Piatti/d'Ambrosio) (1949)
Sonata in G, Op. 2, No. 6 [orig: vlc, b.c.]
  Schott (Gibson) (1911)

Sonata No. 2 in G [orig: vlc, b.c.]
  *Schott (Gibson/Moffat)
Sonatas (2) in *F* and *g* [orig: vlc, b.c.]
  *International (Katims)
Sonatas (2) in *G* and *C* [orig: vlc, b.c.]
  *International (Vieland)
Sonatas (2) in *G* and *e* [orig: vlc, b.c.]
  Schott
Sonatina [vla, pno or vln, pno or vlc, pno]
  *Etling (Etling) (1971)

MARCKHL, Erich (1902-   )

  Music (1941)
    Ms
  Sonata (1939)
    Ms

MARÉCHAL, Henri-Charles (1842-1924)

  Elegy
    Senart (1931)

MARIE, Gabriel (1852-1928)

  La Cinquantaine
    *Billaudot
  Serenade badine
    *Billaudot

MARIE ELISABETH, Princess of Sachsen-Meiningen

  Wiegenlied
    Leuckart (Dessauer) (1894)

MARINI, Carlo Antonio (ca. 1671-   ?)

  Sonata in D [vla, hpscd or vla, pno; orig: vln, b.c.]
    *Doblinger (Stierhof/Hüber)

MAROS, Rudolf (1917-)

Albanian Suite
  *Budapest

MARTEAU, Henri (1874-1934)

Chaconne, Op. 8
  *SimBenjRaht (1905)
Feuillet d'album in d [orig: vln, pno]
  Alsbach (1907)

MARTELLI, Henri (1895-)

Concertstück
  *Ricordi
Sonata
  *Choudens

MARTINI, Giovanni Battista (1706-1784)

Celebrated Gavotte
  *Kjos
Gavotte
  Schott(London)

MARTINI, Jean Paul Égide (1741-1816)

Plaisir d'amour
  Durand (van Waefelghem)

MARTINN, J.

Sonatas
  Frey

MARTINON, Jean Francisque Étienne (1910-1976)

Rapsodie 72
  *Billaudot (1972)

MARTINŮ, Bohuslav (1890-1959)

Rhapsody Concerto (1954)
*Bärenreiter (Sommer) (1972)
Sonata No. 1 (1955)
*Associated (Fuchs)
Vieweg (1958)

MARTUCCI, Giuseppe (1856-1909)

Canto d'amore, Op. 38, No. 3
*Ricordi (Quaranta/d'Ambrosio) (1941)

MARX, Karl (1897-)

Concerto, Op. 10
Bote&Bock (1931)

MASCAGNI, Pietro (1863-1945)

Siciliana
Fischer

MASSENET, Jules Émile Frédéric (1842-1912)

Elegy, from *Les Erynnies*, Op. 10 [orig: orch]
*Fischer (Deery)

MASSIS, Amable (1893-)

Poème [orig: vla, orch]
*Billaudot

MATTHISON-HAUSEN, Gottfred

Sonata in F, Op. 16 [orig: vlc, pno]
Breitkopf (Krall)

MATYS, Jiri (1927-)

Sonata, Op. 16 (1954)
*Artia (1958)

MATZ, Arnold (1904-)

Mixolydian Sonatina
*Peters (1952)
Theme and Variations
*Breitkopf (Baer) (1954)

MAÜGUE, J.M.L.

Allegro, Lento, Scherzo [orig: vla, orch]
Lemoine (1927)
Cantilène and Dance
Lemoine (1928)

MAURAT, Edmond

Caprices originaux (5), Op. 8
*Eschig

MAURER, Louis Wilhelm (1789-1878)

Divertimento, Op. 85 [orig: vla, str orch]
Peters (1861)

MAURY, Lowndes (1911-)

Song Without Words
*Artransa

MAYER, Rudolf (1893-)

Kleine Suite (1938)
*Doblinger (1953)

MAYEUR, L.

Pieces (2)
    Fromont

MAYR, Sebastian

Am Morgen: Idyll [orig: vln, pno]
    Oertel (1898)

MAZAS, Jacques Féréol (1782-1849)

Character Pieces (2) [orig: vln, pno]
    Kreyer (Abbass) (1887)
La Consolation: Elégie in G, Op. 29 [orig: vla, orch]
    Pleyel (1831)
Le Songe: Fantaisie, Op. 92 [orig: vla d'amore, pno]
    Simrock (1855)

MAZELLIER, Jules (1879-1959)

Nocturne and Rondeau
    *Billaudot
    Costallat

MEDIN, Nino (1904-1969)

Entrats, *Largo*, and *Finale*
    pub by comp (1958?)

MEDTNER, Nikolaï Karlovich (1880-1951)

Fairy Tale, Op. 51, No. 3 [orig: pno]
    *Zimmermann

MÉHUL, Étienne Nicolas (1763-1817)

Gavotte
    Schott (Tertis) (1912)

Menuett in A, from *Sonata*, Op. 1, No. 3 [orig: pno]
   Schott(London)

MEJO, W.

Concertino in C [orig: vla, str orch]
   Häcker (1840)

MELLERS, Wilfred Howard (1914-)

Sonata in C (1946)
   *Lengnick (1949)

MENASCE, Jacques de (1905-)

Sonata in One Movement
   *Durand (1956)

MENDELSSOHN, Arnold Ludwig (1855-1933)

Student Concerto in D, Op. 213 [orig: vlc, orch]
   Junne (1908)

MENDELSSOHN-BARTHOLDY, Felix (1809-1847)

Canzonetta, from *String Quartet No. 1 in E-flat*, Op. 12
   Hofmeister (Wittmann) (1871)
Frühlingslied, from *Lieder ohne Worte*, Op. 62, No. 6 [orig: pno]
   Seeling (1888)
Herbstlied, Op. 84, No. 2 [orig: voice, pno]
   Ms (Borisovsky)
Kinderstücke (6), Op. 72 [orig: pno]
   Augener (Kreuz) (1895)
   Schott (1912)
Lied ohne Worte, Op. 38, No. 2 [orig: pno]
   *Augener
   Breitkopf
Lied ohne Worte in G, Op. 62, No. 1 [orig: pno]
   Oxford (Forbes) (1948)

Lied ohne Worte in D, Op. 109 [orig: vlc, pno]
  *International (Katims)
Lieder ohne Worte (2)
  *Chester (Forbes)
Lieder ohne Worte, 7 Favourites [orig: pno]
  Augener (Kreuz) (1930)
Lieder ohne Worte (6), Op. 19, No. 1; Op. 30, No. 4; Op. 38, Nos. 1 &
  2; Op. 53, Nos. 1 & 2 [orig: pno]
  Simrock (Hetsch)
Sonata in c
  *DeutschVerMus (Websky)
Sonata in D, Op. 58 [orig: vlc, pno]
  *Augener
Sonata in f, Op. 4 ("Adieu à Berlin") [orig: vln, pno]
  *Augener
Wedding March, from *A Midsummer Night's Dream*, Op. 61 [orig: orch]
  Breitkopf (Hermann)

MERIGHI, Vincenzo (1795- ?)

Concertino in D [orig: vla, orch]
  Ricordi

MERKEL, Gustav Adolf (1827-1885)

Abendruhe, Op. 50, No. 2 [orig: pno]
  Schott

MERWART, Joseph

Sehnsucht, Op. 8
  pub by comp

METZLER, Wolfgang

Partita on the Chorale "Die Sonn' hat sich mit ihrem Glanz gewendet"
  [vla, org or vla, pno]
  *Hänssler

MEULEMANS, Arthur (1884-1966)
  Concerto (1942)
    *Belgian
  Sonata (1953)
    *Belgian (1956)

MEYER, Clemens (1868-)
  Menuett [orig: vln, pno]
    Benjamin (1896)
  Romance, Op. 6 [orig: vla, orch]
    Benjamin (1896)
  Wiegenlied
    SchmidtCF (Klemcke)

MEYER, Ernst Herman (1905-)
  Poem (1962) [orig: vla, orch]
    *Breitkopf

MEYERBEER, Giacomo (1791-1864)
  Aria, from *Les Huguenots* [orig: voice, orch]
    Augener

MEYER-OLBERSLEBEN, Max (1850-1927)
  Concerto, Op. 112
    Schuberth
  Sonata in C, Op. 14
    Schuberth (1881)

MIASKOVSKII, Nikolaĭ IAkovlevich (1881-1950)
  Sonata No. 2, Op. 81
    Musgis
    RussSt (1951)

MICHIELS, G.

> *Erster Czardas über ungarische Lieder*
> Junne

MIGOT, Georges (1891-)

> *Dialogue in 4 Parts* [orig: vlc, pno]
> Leduc (1952)
> *Le Premier livre de divertissements français à 2 et à 3. No. 4: Estampie*
> [orig: clar, harp]
> *Leduc
> *Second Dialog* [orig: vlc, pno]
> Leduc (1954)

MIHALOVICI, Marcel (1898-)

> *Sonata No. 2*, Op. 45
> Heugel (1954)
> *Sonata in E-flat*, Op. 47
> *Heugel (1948)

MIHÁLY, András (1917-)

> *Rhapsody*
> *Budapest

MILANDRE, Louis Toussaint

> *Suite in D* [vla, pno or vla d'amore, hpscd]
> *Billaudot
> Costallat

MILETIĆ, Miroslav (1925-)

> *Rhapsody*
> Naklada

MILHAUD, Darius (1892-1974)

La Bruxelloise, from *Quatre visages* (1943)
    *Heugel (1946)
La Californienne, from *Quatre visages* (1943)
    *Heugel (1946)
Concerto (1929)
    *Universal (1931)
Concerto No. 2
    *Heugel (1958)
La Parisienne, from *Quatre visages* (1943)
    *Heugel (1946)
Sonata No. 1, on 18th-Century Themes (1944)
    *Heugel
Sonata No. 2 (1944)
    *Heugel (1946)
The Wisconsonian, from *Quatre visages* (1943)
    *Heugel (1946)

MILLER, Michael

Miniatures (3)
    *Hinrichsen

MINE, [?]

Airs varies (3)
    Petit

MOHLER, Philipp Heinrich (1908-)

Konzertante Sonate, Op. 31
    *Schott (1953)

MOJSISOVICS, Roderich von (1877-1953)

Sonata in c, Op. 74
    Krenn (ca. 1961)
    Schuberth (1927)

MOLBE, Heinrich (1835- ?)
Reverie, Op. 35
   Hofmeister (1896)

MONASIPOV, A
Romance
   *MezhdKniga

MONIUSZKO, Stanislaw (1819-1872)
Romance in a
   André (Ritter)
Scene and Romance, from *Halka* [orig: voice, orch]
   Bessel
   Bote&Bock

MONTEUX, Pierre (1875-1964)
Arabesque
   *Salabert
Melody
   *Salabert

MOÓR, Emanuel (1863-1931)
Prelude, Op. 123
   *International (Katims)

MOORE, John Herbert
Elegy
   Stainer (1911)

MORTARI, Virgilio (1902-)
Concerto dell'osservanza
   *Ricordi

MOSER, Rudolf (1892-1960)

    Suite, Op. 81

       Ms

MOSSOLOV, Alexander Vassilievich (1900-)

    Esquisses (3), Op. 2

       Ms

MOULE-EVANS, David (1905-)

    Moto perpetuo

       Williams

MOURANT, Walter (1910-)

    Fantasy

       *AmCompAll

MOUSSORGSKY, Modeste. *See* Musorgskiĭ, Modest Petrovich

MOZART, Johann Chrysostom Wolfgang Amadeus (1756-1791)

    Adagio in C, K. 356 [orig: harmonica]

       Oxford (Forbes) (1952)

    Adagio in D [orig: vln, pno]

       Augener (Woolhouse) (1880)

    Adagio in E, K. 261, and *Rondo in C*, K. 373 [orig: vln, orch]

       Oxford (Forbes/Richardson) (1952)

    Andante (*Ave Maria*), from *Vesperae solemnes de confessore*, K. 339

       [orig: voice, orch]

       Universal (Venzl) (1890)

    Andante, from *String Quintet in C*, K. 515

       Breitkopf (Naumann) (1859)

    Concerto in E-flat

       SAEM (Stolz)

Concerto in A, K. 622 [orig: clar, orch]
    *Chester (Tertis)
    *International (Vieland)
    *MezhdKniga (Strakhov)
Concerto No. 1 in D, K. 412 [orig: hn, orch]
    Breitkopf (Kling/Marchet)
Concerto No. 3 in E-flat, K. 447 [orig: hn, orch]
    *MezhdKniga (Strakhov)
Concerto No. 3 in G, K. 216 [orig: vln, orch]
    *International (Fuchs)
Concerto No. 4 in D, K. 218 [orig: vln, orch]
    *International (Fuchs)
Divertimento in C
    *Elkan-Vogel (Piatigorsky/Elkan)
Gavotte, from *Idomeneo* [orig: orch]
    Bote&Bock (1910)
Ländler
    *Boston (Caruthers)
    Schott(London)
Larghetto, from *Clarinet Quintet in A*, K. 581
    Schott (Kross) (1915)
Laudate Dominum, from *Vesperae solemnes de confessore*, K. 339
    [orig: voice, orch]
    Gebauer (Bockmann) (1884)
Menuet and Trio
    *Chester (Radmall)
Menuett in C
    *Schott (Forbes)
Minuet, from *Divertimento No. 2*, K. 229 [orig: 2 clar, bsn]
    Schott (Forbes) (1957)
Sonata in e, K. 304 [orig: vln, pno]
    *International (Vieland)
    *Peters (Forbes)
Sonatina in A
    Elkan-Vogel (Piatigorsky/Elkan)
Sonatina in C [vla, pno or vln, pno or vlc, pno]
    *Etling (Etling) (1971)
Sonatina No. 1 in F
    *ElkanH (Courte)

Sonatina No. 2 in E-flat
 *ElkanH (Courte)
Sonatina No. 3 in G
 *ElkanH (Courte)
Tonstücke (3)
 Rieter

MÓŽI, Aladar (1923-)

Rapsódia na záhorácke motívy
 *Slovenský

MÜLLER, August Eberhard (1767-1817)

Romance pathétique
 Oertel (Pagels) (1898)

MUELLER, Frederick (1921-)

Andante cantabile
 *Kjos
At the Ballet
 *Kjos
At the Masquerade
 *Kjos
Carnival Time
 *Kjos
Gavotte parisienne
 *Kjos
In a Country Garden
 *Kjos
Lake Champlain Waltz
 *Kjos
Maid of Honor
 *Kjos
Neapolitan Dance
 *Kjos
On the Beach
 *Kjos

La Petite soubrette
  *Kjos
Sleigh Ride Party
  *Kjos
Summertime
  *Kjos
Valse caprice
  *Kjos
Viola Caprice
  *Kjos
Woodland Caprice
  *Kjos

MÜLLER, J. V.

Abend-Andacht: Adagio, Op. 9
  Schott (1884)

MÜLLER, Otto (1837- ?)

Grosses Duo in E-flat, Op. 11
  Cranz (1872)

MÜLLER, Robert

Barkarole, Op. 13, No. 1 [orig: vln, pno]
  Neldner (1901)

MÜLLER-ZÜRICH, Paul (1898-)

Concerto in f, Op. 24
  *Schott

MÜNCHHAUSEN, August Baron von

Sonata, Op. 8
  Schott (ca. 1815)

MÜNTZING, Arne (1903-)

Sonata (1957)
Svenska

MURRILL, Herbert Henry (1909-1952)

French Nursery Songs (4)
*Chester
Sarabande: A Christmas Greeting for Pau Casals [vla, pno or vln, pno or vlc, pno]
Ms

MUSORGSKIĬ, Modest Petrovich (1839-1881)

Hopak [orig: voice, pno or voice, orch]
*Etling (Etling) (1971)
RussSt (Borisovsky) (1936)
Die Träne [orig: voice, pno]
Urbánek (Moravec) (1935)

MUZIO, Emanuele (1825-1890)

Andante
Ricordi (1858)
Rondoletto
Ricordi (1858)

MYLIUS, Hermann

Suite in c, Op. 30 (1939)
*Breitkopf (1954)

NARDINI, Pietro (1722-1793)

Adagio cantabile
Jurgenson
Concerto No. 10 in g [orig: vln, orch]
Oxford (Forbes/Richardson) (1950)

Larghetto [orig: vln, b.c.]
   Steingräber
Sonata in D [orig: vln, b.c.]
   *International (Katims)
Sonata in f [orig: vln, b.c.]
   *Cranz
   *International (Zellner)
Sonata No. 1 in B-flat [orig: vln, b.c.]
   *International (Alard/Dessauer)

NAUMANN, Ernst (1832-1910)

   Fantasie-Stücke (3), Op. 5
      Rieter (1878)
   Sonata in g, Op. 1
      Breitkopf (1855)

NEDBAL, Oskar (1874-1930)

   Romantisches Stück, Op. 18 [orig: vlc, pno]
      Doblinger (Konrath)

NEMEROWSKI, A.

   Méditation, Op. 8
      Jurgenson (Baratynsky)

NERUDA, Franz Xaver (1843-1915)

   Berceuse slave d'après un chant polonais [prog: vln, pno]
      Rahter (Dessauer)

NESSLER, Victor E. (1841-1890)

   Der Rattenfänger von Hameln
      Schuberth

NEUMANN, Věroslav (1931-)

Hudba
*Panton (r)

NEY, Casimir

Etude d'expression
Costallat
Preludes in All Keys (24)
Costallat

NIGGELING, Willi (1924-)

Sonata
*Mitteldeutscher
Peters

NITSCHMANN, Heinrich

Frühlingsbotschaft, Op. 7
Challier (1889)
Lebewohl: Notturno, Op. 9 [orig: vlc, pno]
Challier

NIVERD, Lucien (1879-)

Concerto romantique
Nicosias (1899)

NORMAN, Ludwig (1831-1885)

Sonata in g, Op. 32
Kistner (1875)

NOSSEK, Karl

Chanson du berceau, Op. 21 [orig: vln, pno]
Oertel

Im einsamen Fischerkahn. Seul! En Bateau. Barcarolle, Op. 27 [orig:
vln, pno]
    Oertel (1898)
Près du léman. Abend an Genfer See. Rêverie, Op. 28 [orig: vla, str orch]
    Oertel (1898)
Speranza: Salonstück, Op. 25
    Oertel (1898)

NOVÁK, Jan (1921-)

Suite, Op. 28 (1951)
    Ms

NOWAK, Lionel (1911-)

Duo
    *AmCompAll

NUSSIO, Otmar (1902-)

Notturno di Valdemosa
    *Universal

OERTEL, August

Wiegenlied, Op. 5 [orig: vln, pno]
    Heinrichshofen

OLIVE, Joseph

Episodes (7)
    *AmCompAll

OLIVIER, François (1907-)

Suite
    Universal (1953)

ONSLOW, Georges (1784-1853)

Sonata, Op. 16, No. 1 [vla, pno or vlc, pno]
Breitkopf (ca. 1820)

Sonata in c, Op. 16, No. 2 [vla, pno or vlc, pno]
*Bärenreiter (Wegner) (1972)
Breitkopf (ca. 1820)

Sonata in A, Op. 16, No. 3 [vla, pno or vlc, pno]
Breitkopf (ca. 1820)
*SimBenjRaht (Höckner)

ORR, Robin (1909-)

Sonata
Oxford (Forbes) (1949)

ORREGO-SALAS, Juan Antonio (1919-)

Mobili, Op. 63
*Peer-Southern (1971)

ORTHEL, Léon (1905-)

Sonata, Op. 52
*Donemus

ORTIZ, Diego (ca. 1525- ?)

Doulce memoire
*MCA (Berger)

OSIECK, Hans Hendrik Willem (1910-)

Sonatina (1952)
*Donemus (1952)

OSTERC, Slavko (1895-1941)

Sonata
Ms

OSTERGREN, Eduardo
    Sonata in Three Centuries
    *Fema

OTTEN, Ludwig (1924-)
    Sonata (1953)
    *Donemus (1957)

OVERTON, Hall (1920-1972)
    Sonata
    *AmCompAll

PAGANINI, Niccolò (1782-1840)
    La Companella [orig: vln, orch]
        *Schott (Primrose)
    Caprice, Op. 1, No. 24 [orig: vln solo]
        *Fischer (Primrose)
    Caprices, Op. 1, Nos. 13 and 20 [orig: vln solo]
        *Hinrichsen (Forbes/Richardson)
    Moto perpetuo, Op. 11 [orig: vln, orch]
        *International (Vieland)

PAGIN, André Noël (1721- ?)
    Sonata No. 5 in A [orig: vln, b.c.]
        Schott

PAKETURAS, V.
    Variations
        Ms

PALASCHKO, Johannes (1877-)
    Jagdstück, Op. 36 [orig: vla solo]
        Kistner (1912)

Melodische Etuden, Op. 92
Simrock (1929)

PALKOVSKÝ, Oldřich (1907-)

Sonata No. 2
*Panton (r)

PALMER, Robert (1915-)

Sonata (1948)
*Peer-Southern

PAPANDOPULO, Boris (1906-)

Sonata
*DruštvoHS

PAÔUE, Désiré

Suite de danse, Op. 46
Muraille (1910)
Suites (4), Op. 15, 20, 26, 27
Ms

PARADIES, Pietro Domenico (1707-1791)

Canzonetta
Schott (London)
Toccata in C [vla, pno or vln, pno]
Oxford (Forbes) (1957)

PARISOT, Octave

Un Rêve: Melodie [orig: vln, pno]
Costallat

PARRIS, Robert (1924-   )

Sonata (1957)
   *AmCompAll

PARROTT, Ian (1916-   )

Aquarelle
   *Chester

PARTOS, Oedoen (1907-   )

Oriental Ballad
   *IsMusPub
Sinfonia concertante: Concerto No. 3
   *IsMusInst
Yiskor [orig: vla, orch]
   *IsMusPub

PASCAL, André

Chant sans paroles
   *Durand (1925)

PASMORE, H. B.

Barkarole [orig: vlc, pno]
   Bote&Bock

PAUDERT, Ernst

Lieder ohne Worte
   Benjamin

PAUL, Alan (1905-1968)

Sonata
   *Bosworth (1948)

PEARSON, William Dean (1905-)

Carols (2)
*Hinrichsen

PEIXE, César Guerra (1914-)

Miniatures (1958)
Ms
Pieces (3) (1957)
Ms

PEJAN, A.

Sonatina
Ms

PELEMANS, Willem (1901-)

Serenade en dans (1947)
Belgian
Maurer
Sonata No. 2 (1946)
Belgian
Maurer
Walzersonate (1949)
Belgian
Maurer (1956)

PENN, William A. (1943-)

Chamber Music I
*AmCompAll

PENTLAND, Barbara (1912-)

Duo (1960)
*Canadian (loan)

PEPUSCH, John Christopher (1667-1752)
Largo and Allegro in d
    *Broekmans

PERGAMENT, Moses (1893-   )
Duo, Op. 28
    Nordiska

PERGOLESI, Giovanni Battista (1710-1736)
Arietta
    *Chester (Radmall) (1952)
Se tu m'ami
    *ElkanH (Elkan)

PERILHOU, A.
Menuet [orig: vln, pno]
    Heugel
Scènes agrestas: 1. Danse rustique
    Heugel

PERLE, George (1915-   )
Preludio, Invention, and *Ostinato*
    InstIntMus
Sonata (1949)
    InstIntMus
Sonata, Op. 12
    InstIntMus (1954)

PERROTA, Vinceno
Sonata
    Ricordi (1938)
Sonatina
    Ricordi

PERSICHETTI, Vincent (1915-)

Infanta marina, Op. 83 (1960)
*Elkan-Vogel

PETROVA, Elena Pavlovna

Sonata
*Panton (r)

PETTERSON, A.

Album Leaf
Vincent (1898)

PFEIFFER, August

Wiegenlied (*Berceuse*), Op. 6 [orig: vln, pno]
Rühle

PIANTONI, Louis (1885-1958)

Dance
Ms
Pieces (3)
Ms
Sonata No. 1
Ms
Sonata No. 2
Ms

PIATTI, Alfredo (1822-1901)

Supplication [orig: vlc, pno]
Brockhaus

PIERNÉ, Henri-Constant-Gabriel (1863-1937)

Sérénade, Op. 7 [orig: pno]
*Leduc (Neuberth)
Williams (Tertis) (1908)

Solo de concert, Op. 35 [orig: bsn, pno]
    Buffet (Neuberth)

PILATI, Mario (1903-1938)
    Inquiétude [orig: vlc, pno]
        Leduc (1931)

PINEDA-DUQUE, Roberto (1910-   )
    Sonata (1957)
    Ms

PISK, Paul Amadeus (1893-   )
    Movements (3), Op. 36
        *AmCompAll

PISTON, Walter Hamor (1894-1976)
    Concerto (1957)
        *Associated
    Interlude (1942)
        *Boosey (1952)

PISTOR, Carl Friedrich (1884-   )
    Heitere Musik, Op. 69
    Ms

PITTFIELD, Thomas Baron (1903-   )
    Sonatas (2) *in E* and *G*, Op. 9
        International
    Sonatina
        *Cramer

PIZZETTI, Ildebrando (1880-1968)

Sonata in F [orig: vlc, pno]
Ricordi (Corti)

PLANEL, Robert (1908-)

Fantasy
*Leduc

PLAVEC, Josef (1905-)

Liebreiche (1942)
Ms
Meditation (1934)
Ms

PLEYEL, Ignaz Joseph (1757-1831)

Concerto in D, Op. 31
*Grahl (Hermann) (1951)

PODÉŠT, Ludvik (1921-1968)

Suite (1956)
*Artia (Hyska) (1958)

POENITZ, Franz

Idylle (*Weihnachtsstück*), Op. 23
Simon

POGGE, Hans

Sonata in F, Op. 14 [orig: clar, pno]
Eulenburg (1912)

POLAK-DANIELS, B.

Morceaux de salon (2), Op. 86
Bellmann

PONCE, Manuel María (1882-1948)

Estrellita
*Fischer

POPPER, David (1843-1913)

Romance, Op. 32
*Augener

PORPORA, Nicola Antonio (1686-1767?)

Aria
Chester
Sonata in G [orig: vln, hpscd]
Breitkopf (Hermann)
*International (David/Hermann)
Sonata No. 9 in E [orig: vln, hpscd]
*International (Alard/Dessauer)
Schott (Dessauer)
Sonata No. 11 in D [orig: vln, hpscd]
Costallat

PORTER, Quincy (1897-1966)

Blues lontaines
*AmCompAll
Concerto (1948)
*Associated
Duo (1957) [vla, harp or vla, hpscd]
*Associated
Poem [vla, pno or vlc, pno]
*NewValley

Speed Etude
*NewValley

POUWELS, Jan (1898-)
Sonata (1955)
*Donemus (1955)

POVIA, F.
Elegy
Naklada

PRATELLA, Francesco Balilla (1880-1955)
Sonata No. 1 [orig: vln, pno]
Bongiovanni (Pasi) (1921)

PROCH, Heinrich (1809-1878)
Thème varié, Op. 164
Costallat

PROKOF'EV, Sergeï Sergeevich (1891-1953)
Selected Pieces, from *Romeo and Juliet* [orig: orch]
*MezhdKniga (Borisovsky)
Theme and Processional, from *Peter and the Wolf* [orig: orch]
*Omega (Grunes)

PROUT, Ebenezer (1835-1909)
Romance in F, Op. 32
Augener (1900)
Sonata in D, Op. 26
Augener

PURCELL, Henry (ca. 1659-1695)

Air
Schott (Moffat)
Air, *Dance*, and *Ground*, from *Dido and Aeneas* [orig: orch]
*Belwin-Mills (Lutyens)
Chester
Aria
*International (Katims)
Bourrée and Hornpipe
*Chester (Forbes) (1956)
Schottisches Lied und Tanz
*Chester (Radmall)
Sonata in g [orig: vln, b.c.]
*Oxford (Forbes/Richardson)
Suite of Airs and Dances
*International (Vieland)

PYCHOWSKI, J. N.

Duetto dramatico, Op. 18 [orig: clar, pno]
Schuberth (1856)

QUANTZ, Johann Joachim (1697-1773)

Sonata in a [vla, b.c.]
Breitkopf (1762)

QUARANTA, Felice (1910-   )

Sonata
Ms

QUINET, Fernand (1898-   )

Sonata in C
Senart (1928)

QUINET, Marcel (1915-)

   Concerto
   *Belgian

RACHMANINOFF, Sergei (1873-1943)

   Barcarolle, Op. 10, No. 3 [orig: pno]
      Ricordi (d'Ambrosio) (1923)
   Mélodie and Sérénade, Op. 3, Nos. 3 and 5 [orig: pno]
      Hamelle (1935)
   Prelude, Op. 23, No. 4 [orig: pno]
      *MezhdKniga (Borisovsky)
   Sonata in g, Op. 19 [orig: vlc, pno]
      Ms (Borisovsky) (1933)

RADNAI, Miklos (1892-1935)

   Sonata in d, (1913)
      Hofmeister
      Simrock (1919)

RAFF, Joseph Joachim (1822-1882)

   Cavatina [orig: vln, pno]
      *Fischer (Ritter/Schloming)
   Morceaux de salon (6), Op. 85 [orig: pno]
      *Augener

RAFFER, Leonard (1911-1965)

   Pieces (5)
      *Bosworth

RAINIER, Priaulx (1903-)

   Sonata (1945)
      *Schott (1949)

RAMEAU, Jean Philippe (1683-1764)

Pieces for Viola, 4 vols.
*Budapest (Horvsitzky/Tatrai)
Rigaudon in d
*Belwin-Mills (Applebaum)
Suite of 3 Dances
*Oxford (Forbes/Richardson)
La Villageoise, from *Pièces de claveçin* (1724) [orig: hpscd]
   Schott (Moffat)

RAMIREZ, Luis Antonio

Meditacion à la memoria de Segundo Ruiz Delvis (1973)
*Seesaw

RAMOVŠ, Primož (1921-)

Aformizmi (Aphorisms)
*Društva
Nokturno
*Društva
Skice (Sketches)
*Društva

RAMSOE, Wilhelm (1837- ?)

Romance in D, Op. 28
   Hansen (ca. 1905)

RAPHAEL, Günter Albert Rudolf (1903-1960)

Sonata in E-flat, Op. 13 (1926)
*Breitkopf (1955)
Sonata No. 2, Op. 80 (1954)
*Breitkopf (1957)

RAPOPORT, Eda (1900-)

Poem
*Mercury

RATEZ, Émile-Pierre (1851-1934)

Sonata in E-flat, Op. 48 (1907)
Breitkopf
Rouart (1907)

RATTI, Lorenzo (1590-1630)

Sonata in A [vla, b.c.]
Breitkopf (1762)
Sonata in D [vla, b.c.]
Breitkopf (1762)

RAUNICK, W.

Klage in a, Op. 42 [orig: vlc, pno]
Simon (1899)
Tröstung in E, Op. 43 [orig: vln, pno]
Simon (1899)

RAVEL, Maurice (1875-1937)

Pavane pour une infante défunte [orig: pno]
*Eschig (Kochanski)
Schott
Piece en forme d'habanera [orig: voice, pno]
*Leduc
Marks

RAWSTHORNE, Alan (1905-1971)

Sonata (1937; rev. 1954)
Oxford (1955)

READ, Gardner (1913-)

Fantasy, Op. 38 [orig: vla, orch]
Associated

Poem, Op. 31a (1934) [vla, pno or hn, pno; orig: vla, orch]
*Fischer

REBER, Horst

Berceuse celebre, Op. 15, No. 5
*Billaudot

REBIKOV, Vladimir Ivanovitch (1866-1920)

Berceuse and Dance
*Chester (Forbes)
Lied ohne Worte
Musgis (1951)
Without Thee
Fischer

REBLING, Gustav (1821-1902)

Sonata in g, Op. 22 [orig: vlc, pno]
Heinrichshofen (1866)

REBNER, Edward Wolfgang (1910-)

Virtuose Legende [orig: vla, orch]
*Moderne

RÉE, Louis (1861-1939)

Melody, Op. 22, No. 1 [orig: pno]
Robitschek (1897)

REED, Alfred (1921-)

Rhapsody [orig: vla, orch]
*Boosey

REED, William Henry (1876-1942)

Rhapsody
Augener (1927)

REED, William Leonard (1910-)

Suite, "The Top Flat" (1947)
Ms

REGER, Max (1873-1916)

Romance in G [orig: pno]
*Breitkopf (Sitt)
Sonata No. 3 in B-flat, Op. 107 [orig: clar, pno]
*Bote&Bock

REICHEL, Bernard (1901-)

Sonata
Ms
Sonatina
Ms

REINECKE, Karl Heinrich Carsten (1824-1910)

Fantasiestücke (3), Op. 43
Breitkopf (1857)
Petits morceaux (10), Op. 122
*Augener (Kreuz)
Petits morceaux (10), Op. 213
*Augener (Kreuz)
Sonata in A, Op. 42 [orig: vlc, pno]
Fürstner (1857)

REINHOLD, Otto (1899-1965)

Music
*Bärenreiter (1952)

REITER, Albert (1905-   )
Sonata
  *Doblinger

REIZENSTEIN, Franz Theodore (1911-1968)
  Concert Fantasy, Op. 42
  *Hinrichsen

RENDALL, Homer
  Pieces (2)
  Williams (1950)

RENDSBURG, Jacques E.
  Am Meeresstrande, Op. 4 [orig: vlc, pno]
  Breitkopf (1892)

RENOSTO, Paolo (1935-   )
  Avant d'ecrire
  *Ricordi

RENTSCH, Ernst
  Romance, Op. 6 [orig: vln, pno]
  Hug (Dessauer) (1894)

RESCH, C.
  Serenade
  Laudy (1887)

RESSI, M.
  Sonata, Op. 5
  Ricordi

RETTICH, Wilhelm (1892-   )

Suite in the Old Style, Op. 40c [orig: vla, str orch]
*Novello

REUCHSEL, Maurice (1880-1968)

Caprice de concert
Hamelle (1914)

REUTTER, Hermann (1900-   )

Music (1951)
Associated
*Schott (1952)

RIBÁRI, Antal (1924-   )

Sonata
*Budapest (Lukács)

RIBOLLET, A.

Suite, Op. 23
Costallat
Leduc (1924)

RICCIUS, August Ferdinand (1819-   ?)

Introduction and Allegro, Op. 18
Ries&Erler (1853)

RICHARDS, Brinley (1817-1885)

God Bless the Prince of Wales
*Augener (Hermann)

RICHARDSON, Alan (1904-   )

Autumn Sketches
   Oxford (Forbes) (1949)
Intrada
   Oxford (Forbes)
Sonata, Op. 21
   Augener (Forbes) (1955)
Sussex Lullaby
   Oxford (Forbes) (1938)

RICHTER, Marga (1926-   )

Air and Toccata [orig: vla, str orch]
   *Belwin-Mills

RIEGER, Otto (1892-   )

Sonata in F
   Doblinger (1924)

RIES, Ferdinand (1784-1838)

Kleine und leichte Vortragsstücke (6)
   Schmid (1894)

RIES, Franz (1846-1932)

Adagio, Op. 34, No. 3
   Ries&Erler
Romance, Op. 27, No. 4
   Ries&Erler

RIFFAUD, L.

Impromptu in D-flat, Op. 2
   Costallat (1910)
Nocturne in c-sharp, Op. 7
   Costallat (1910)

RIHA, Oldrich

Suite
    Ms

RIMSKII-KORSAKOV, Nikolai Andreevich (1844-1908)
Dance of the Buffoons, from *Snow Maiden* [orig: orch]
    *MezhdKniga (Strakhov)
Song of India, from *Sadko* [orig: voice, orch]
    *Fischer (Deery)

RITTER, Alexander (1833-1896)
Tonstück
    Universal (Ritter) (1901)

RITTER, Hermann (1849-1926)
Dithyrambe, Op. 74
    Kistner (1907)
Elfengesang, Op. 7
    Simrock (1883)
Erinnerung an Schottland, Op. 34
    Kistner (1886)
Gesangsstück, Op. 66
    SchmidtCF (1900)
Italian Suite, Op. 37 (1886)
    Kistner
Jagdstück, Op. 17
    Simrock (1883)
Melody
    Schmid (1878)
Ständchen, Op. 70
    Kistner (1905)
Stücke (2), Op. 32
    Kistner (1886)
Stücke (2), Op. 48
    Hofmeister (1889)

Stücke (2), Op. 65
    Kistner (1898)
Stücke (2), *nach slawischen Eindrücken*, Op. 33
    Kistner (1886)
Vortragsstücke (2), Op. 73
    Kistner (1907)

RIVIER, Jean (1896-)

Concertino [orig: vla, orch]
    *Senart
Doloroso et giocoso
    *Billaudot

ROBBINS, L.

Petite suite [orig: vln, pno]
    Bosworth (1912)

ROBBRECHTS, Andre (1797- ?)

Mélodie pastorale
    Costallat (ca. 1850)

RODE, Pierre (1774-1830)

Notturno
    Simon
Siciliano, from *Concerto No. 5* [orig: vln, orch]
    Challier (1886)

RÖNTGEN, Johannes (1898-)

Sonata
    *Donemus

RÖTSCHER, Konrad (1910-)

Music, Op. 27
    *Bote&Bock (1954)

ROGER, Kurt George (1895-1966)

Aria, from *Partita* (1951) [orig: vlc, pno]
Ms
Irish Sonata, Op. 37 (1939)
Francis (1948)
Lengnick
Suite, Op. 84 (1954)
Ms

ROGERS, William Keith (1921-)

Sonatina
*BMICan (1954)
*Canadian (loan)

ROGISTER, Jean (1879-1964)

Concerto No. 1
Ms
Fantaisie concertante
Ms
Fantaisie sur un theme wallon
Ms
Libellule (*Pièce caracteristique*) [vla, pno or vln, pno]
Schott (1949)
Prélude, Adieu, Libellule
Ms

ROGOWSKI, Ludomir Michael (1881-1954)

Conte merveilleux (1916)
Ms

ROHWER, Jens (1914-)

Kleine Sonate in e
Voggenreiter (1944)
Sonata [vla, hpscd or vla, pno]
*Möseler

ROLLA, Alessandro (1757-1841)

Adagio e Tema con Variazioni [orig: vla, orch]
  Günther (Kint)
  *Suvini-Zerboni (Bianchi)
Concerto in E-flat, Op. 3 (2nd version)
  *Belwin-Mills (Beck)
  *Columbo (Beck)
  International
  *Ricordi (Beck)
Concerto in F
  *Santis (Centurioni/Mercatali) (1970)
Concerto in F
  Günther (Schaller/Kint) (1938)
Sonata in A-flat
  *Suvini-Zerboni (Bianchi/Tamponi) (1977)
Sonatas (2), *in E-flat* and *d,* Op. 3
  Artaria
  Costallat
  Richault
  Sieber

ROLLAND, Paul and Fletcher, Stanley

First Perpetual Motion
  *Mills

ROMBERG, Bernhard Heinrich (1767-1841)

Sonata [vla, pno or vln, pno or vlc, pno]
  *Etling (Etling) (1971)

ROSEN, Jerome (1921-)

Pieces (5)
  *AmCompAll

ROSENBERG, Hilding Constantin (1892-)

Concerto (1942)
  *Nordiska

ROSENHAIN, Jacob (1813-1894)

Sonata, Op. 98
Breitkopf

ROSKOSCHNY, Joseph Richard

Solitude [orig: ob, pno]
Oertel (1907)

ROSSI, Achille

Sognando (Dreaming)
Brosio

ROSSLAVETZ, Nikolay Andreyevitch (1881-1944)

Sonata in One Movement (1929)
Ms

ROTER, Nino

Sonata (1933-1934)
Ms

ROUGNON, Paul L. (1846-   ?)

Allegro appassionato
Gallet (1916)
Concerto romantique, Op. 138
*Hamelle
Fantaisie-caprice
*Leduc (1922)
Fantaisie de concert No. 4
*Billaudot

ROUSSE, J.

Largo
Leduc (1912)

ROUSSEAU, Norbert Oscar Claude (1907-   )

Sonatina, Op. 41 (1949)
   *Belgian (1955)

ROUSSEL, Albert Charles Paul (1869-1937)

Aria [orig: vla, orch]
   *Leduc

ROWLEY, Alec (1892-1958)

Aubade; Farandole; Rêverie; Scherzo
   Williams
Lyric Sonata [orig: vlc, pno]
   Stainer (1929)

RUBBRA, Edmund Duncan (1901-   )

Concerto in A, Op. 75
   *Lengnick

RUBENSTEIN, Anton (1829-1894)

Morceaux de salon (3), Op. 11, Nos. 4-6
   *Augener (Hermann)
   *Hamelle
Romance
   *Fox (Cheyette)
Sonata in f, Op. 49
   *Breitkopf (1954)
   Hamelle
   *RussSt (1960)

RUDZINSKI, Witold (1913-   )

Sonata (1946)
   *PolWydMuz (Szaleski) (1949)

RÜDIGER, S.
>   *Concerto No. 1 in C,* Op. 1
>   Simrock

RUEFF, Jeanine (1922-)
>   *Dialogues*
>   *Leduc

RUMMEL, Karl
>   *Variations in F* [orig: bsn, pno]
>   Schott

RUSSELL, [?]
>   *Life on the Ocean Wave*
>   *Kjos

RUSSO, J.
>   *Il Direttore*
>   *ElkanH

RUST, Friedrich Wilhelm (1739-1796)
>   *Sonata in C* [vla, keyboard or vla, 2 hns, vlc]
>   Günther
>   *ProMusica (Janetzky)
>   *Sonatas* (4) [vla, keyboard or vla, 2 hns, vlc]
>   Ms

RUYGROK, Leo (Leonard Petrus) (1889-1944)
>   *Poème, Fantasiestück,* Op. 20 [orig: vla, orch]
>   Breitkopf (1933)

RYELANDT, Joseph (1870-1965)
>   *Sonata,* Op. 73 (1919)
>   *Belgian

SACCO, P. Peter (1928-   )
Sequence
    *Ostara

SACHS, Léo (1856-1930)
Sonata in A, Op. 176
    Senart (1923)

SAIKKOLA, Lauri (1906-   )
Sonatina (1950)
    Ms

SAINT-GEORGE, George (1841-1924)
L'Ancien régime: Suite, Op. 60 [orig: vln, pno]
    Augener (1904)
Berceuse plaintive, Op. 55 [orig: vln, pno]
    Augener (1903)
Chant de mon coeur
    Lemoine
Chant suppliant
    Lemoine
Elégie [orig: vln, pno]
    Woolhouse
Nymphe des bois
    Lemoine

SAINTON, Prosper (1813-1890)
Lament [orig: vln, pno]
    Augener (1926)

SAINT-SAËNS, Camille (1835-1921)
Concerto No. 1 in a, Op. 33 [orig: vlc, orch]
    Durand

Le Cygne, from *Carnival of the Animals* [orig: orch]
   *Fischer (Gottlieb)
   *Paxton (de Smet) (1972)
Suite in d, Op. 16 [orig: vlc, pno]
   *Hamelle (1903)

SALMHOFER, Franz (1900-   )
   Sonata
   Ms

SAMIE, Auguste
   L'Exilé, Op. 2
   Leduc (Raley)

SAMSON, Ludwig
   Fantasiestücke (3), Op. 43
   Reinecke (1893)

SANCHEZ-MÁLAGA, Carlos (1904-   )
   Romance (1928)
   Ms

SANDBY, Herman (1881-   )
   Danish Song [vla, pno or vln, pno or vlc, pno]
      *Etling (Etling) (1971)
      Hansen
   Song of Vermland (Swedish Folk Song) [vla, pno or vln, pno or vlc, pno]
      *Etling (Etling) (1971)

SANDRE, Gustave (1843-   ?)
   Pieces (2), Op. 61
   Leduc (ca. 1898)

Romance in F, Op. 39
  Hamelle (ca. 1885)

SANTORO, Claudio (1919-   )
  Sonata (1943)
  Ms

SANTÓRSOLA, Guido (1904-   )
  Canción triste y Danza brasileña (1934) [vla, pno or vln, pno; orig: vla, orch]
  Ms
  Choro No. 1 (1944) [vln, pno or vla, pno]
  Ms
  Choro No. 3 (1952) [vln, pno or vla, pno]
  Ms
  Sonata (1928) [vln, pno or vla, pno]
  Ms

SAPIEYEVSKI, Jerzy (1945-   )
  Concerto for Viola and Winds (1971)
  *Mercury (1974)

SAPP, Allen Dwight (1922-   )
  Sonata No. 1
  *AmCompAll

SARAI, Tibor (1919-   )
  Humoresque
  *Budapest (Lukács)
  Kultura

SCHAD, Joseph (1812-1879)
  Le Soupir, Op. 19
  Schott

SCHÄFER, Gerhart (1926-)

Espressioni
*SimBenjRaht
Kleine Stücke (4)
*Gerig (1958)

SCHÄFER, Karl (1899-)

Divertimento on a Theme by Conrad Paumann [orig: vla, chamb orch]
*Gerig

SCHAEUBLE, Hans-Joachim (1906-)

Music, Op. 23 (1938-1939) [orig: vla, orch]
*Bote&Bock

SCHARWENKA, Philipp (1847-1917)

Aria, Op. 51
Simon
Sonata in g, Op. 106
Breitkopf (1899)

SCHEER, Leo

Lament
*Seesaw

SCHELB, Josef (1894-)

Sonata
Ms

SCHERENHALS, [?]

Concertino
Schott (ca. 1900)

SCHIBLER, Armin (1920-)

Ballade, Op. 54
Ahn&Sim (1957)

SCHICKELE, Peter (1935-)

Sonata for Viola Four Hands and Harpsichord [vla, hpscd]
*Presser

SCHIFF, Helmut (1893-)

Sonata
*Doblinger

SCHIRINSKIJ, Wassilij Petrowitsch (1901-1965)

Prelude (1920)
Ms
Sonata in c, Op. 4
RussSt (1926)
Sonata No. 2 (1953)
Ms

SCHLÄGER, Hans (1820-1885)

Nachtstück, Op. 32
Lienau (1872)

SCHLEMM, Gustav Adolf (1902-)

Sonata
Ms

SCHLEMÜLLER, Hugo

Our Soldiers (*March*), Op. 12, No. 5
*Fischer

A Prayer
  *Fischer
A Song
  *Fischer

SCHMIDT, C.

Polonaise
  Peters

SCHMIDT, William J. (1926-)

Sonata in Two Movements
  *Avant

SCHMITT, Aloys (1788-1866)

Cantabile, Op. 106
  Hofmeister (1899)

SCHMITT, Florent (1870-1958)

Legende, Op. 66 [orig: vla, orch or sax, orch]
  *Durand (Schmitt)

SCHMITT, Jacob (1803-1853)

Spring Song
  *Belwin-Mills (Applebaum)

SCHOECK, Othmar Gottfried (1886-1957)

Andante [vla, pno or clar, pno]
  *Peters

SCHOENDLINGER, Anton (1919-)

Sonata
  *Breitkopf (1955)

SCHOLLUM, Robert (1913-   )

Chaconne, Op. 54a (1954)
  *Doblinger (1956)
Sonata, Op. 42, No. 2 (1950)
  *Doblinger
Sonatina, Op. 57, No. 2 (1962)
  *Doblinger (1962)

SCHUBERT, Franz (François) (1808-1878)

L'Abeille, Op. 13, No. 9 [orig: vln, pno]
  Ms (Borisovsky)

SCHUBERT, Franz Peter (1797-1828)

Ave Maria, Op. 52 [orig: voice, pno]
  *Schott (Primrose) (1951)
Litanei auf der Fest aller Seelen [orig: voice, pno]
  *Schott (Primrose) (1951)
Prayer, Op. 139 [orig: chor, pno]
  *Oxford (Ferguson)
Reverie, from *Sonata in A*, Op. 120 [orig: pno]
  *Oxford (Forbes)
Romance, from *Rosamunde*, Op. 26 [orig: orch]
  Augener (Thomas) (1894)
Scherzo in B-flat, D. 593, No. 1 [orig: pno]
  RussSt (Borisovsky) (1936)
Schwanengesang, Op. 23, No. 3 [orig: voice, pno]
  Augener (1903)
Serenade
  Augener (Thomas)
Serenade [orig: voice, pno]
  *Galliard
Sonata in a, D. 821 ("Arpeggione") [orig: arpeggione, pno]
  *Doblinger (Platz)
  *International (Katims)
  *Peters (Drechsel)
  *Schirmer (Doktor)

*Schott (Rostal)
Williams (Forbes)
Sonata Movement, D. 471 [orig: vln, vla, vlc]
*Augener (1960)
Sonatina No. 1 in D, Op. 137 [orig: vln, pno]
*International (Ritter)

SCHUBERT, Joseph (1757- ?)
Concerto in C
*Schott (Schultz/Hauser)

SCHUBERT, Louis (1828-1884)

Paraphrase on the Swedish Folksong "Der Hirt vom Berge," Op. 34
[orig: hn, orch]
Forberg (1880)

SCHUBERT, Wilhelm

Maiblümchen: Rêverie russe
Jurgenson

SCHULTZE, Louis

Danse russe: Burleske [vla, pno or vla, chamb orch; orig: vln, pno]
Oertel

SCHUMANN, Robert Alexander (1810-1856)

Abendlied, Op. 85, No. 12 [orig: pno 4 hands]
Ms (Borisovsky)
Adagio and Allegro in A-flat, Op. 70 [orig: hn, pno]
*International (Vieland)
Litolff (Böhme) (1877)
*Peters
*Schirmer [vla, pno or hn, pno or vln, pno or vlc, pno]

Chor der Houris and Arie nebst Schlusschor, from *Das Paradies und die Peri*,
  Op. 50 [orig: voice, chor, orch]
    Breitkopf (Hermann) (1900)
Erinnerung, from *Album für die Jugend*, Op. 68, No. 28 [orig: pno]
    Schott (Moffat) (1930)
Humming Song and Hunting Song, from *Album für die Jugend*, Op. 68,
  Nos. 3 and 7 [orig: pno]
    Augener (Kreuz)
Liederalbum für die Jugend (4), Op. 79 [orig: voice, pno]
    Schott (Kross) (1890)
Märchenbilder (Fairy Tales) (4), Op. 113
    *Breitkopf
    *International
    *Peters (Hermann) [vla, pno or vln, pno]
    *Schirmer (Schradieck) [vla, pno or vln, pno]
Melody and Soldiers' March, Op. 68, Nos. 1 and 2 [orig: pno]
    Augener (Kreuz)
Romance in F-sharp, Op. 28, No. 2 [orig: pno]
    Cramer (Jacobson) (1947)
Romance; *Merry Peasant*
    *Augener
Romances (3), Op. 94 [orig: ob, pno]
    *Augener
Siciliano and ***, from *Album für die Jugend*, Op. 68, Nos. 11 and 26
  [orig: pno]
    Augener (Kreuz)
Stücke im Volkston (5), Op. 102 [orig: vlc, pno]
    *Augener
Traumerei (Dreaming), from *Kinderscenen*, Op. 15, No. 7 [orig: pno]
    *Fischer (Davidoff/Isaac/Lewis)

SCHWARTZ, Elliott S. (1936-)
  Suite (1963)
    Ms

SCHWARZ, Maximillian (1899-)
  Theme and Variations
    *Breitkopf (1954)

SCOTT, Cyril Meir (1879-1970)

Cherry Ripe
Schott (Tertis)
Fantasy
Schott

SCRIABIN, Alexander. *See* Skriabin, Aleksandr Nikolaevich

SEHLBACH, Erich Oswald (1898-)

Kleine Kammermusik
*Möseler

SEIBER, Mátyás György (1905-1960)

Elegy [orig: vla, orch]
*Schott (Banks)

SEITZ, Friedrich

Concerto No. 4 [orig: vln, orch]
*Boston (Caruthers)
Concerto No. 5 in D, Op. 22 (first movement) [orig: vln, orch]
*Mills (Klotman)
Fantaisie de concert, Op. 31
*Leduc
Student Concerto No. 2, Op. 13 [orig: vln, orch]
*Associated (Lifschey)
Student Concerto No. 3, Op. 12 [orig: vln, orch]
*Associated (Lifschey)

SEKLES, Bernhard (1872-1934)

Chaconne über ein achttaktiges Marschthema, Op. 38
Peters (1931)

SENAILLÉ, Jean Baptiste (1687-1730)

Allegro spiritoso
*International (Katims)

Sonata in g, Op. 5, No. 9 [orig: vln, b.c.]
Augener (Morgan)

SENDREY, Albert Richard (1922-   )
Sonata
Elkan-Vogel

SERLY, Tibor (1900-   )
Concerto
Leeds
Rhapsody, on *Folk Songs Harmonized by Béla Bartók* [orig: vla, orch]
*Peer-Southern

SETER, Mordecai (1916-   )
Elegy [orig: vla, orch]
*IsMusInst

SHEBALIN, Vissarion Yakovlevich (1902-1963)
Sonata
GosMusIzd
*MezhdKniga

SHEER, [?]
Lament
*SouthernTX

SHORE, Bernhard Alexander Royle (1896-   )
Scherzo
Augener (1935)

SHOSTAKOVICH, Dmitriĭ Dmitrievich (1906-1975)

Barrel-Organ Waltz; *Nocturne*; *Galop*
　*MezhdKniga (Borisovsky)
Overture; *Romance*; *Contradance*
　*MezhdKniga (Borisovsky)
Sonata in d, Op. 40 [orig: vlc, pno]
　Anglo-Soviet
　Musgis

SHULMAN, Alan (1915-　)

Homage to Erik Satie
　Schirmer (1951)
Theme and Variations (1940) [orig: vla, orch]
　*Chappell

SIEGL, Otto (1896-　)

Sonata No. 1, Op. 41
　*Doblinger (1925)
Sonata No. 2 in E-flat, Op. 103
　*Doblinger (1939)
Weihnachts-Sonate, Op. 137 [vla, org]
　*Doblinger

SIENNICKI, Edmund

Highland Heather
　*Kjos
Woodland Waltz
　Kjos

SIMON, Anton (1851-ca. 1918)

Berceuse [orig: vln, pno]
　Junne

SIMONETTI, Achille (1857-1928)

Allegretto romantique
   Chester (1898)
Ballata
   Chester (1898)

SIMONS, Netty (1913-)

Facets No. 3 (1962) [vla, pno or ob, pno]
   Merion

SIRULNIKOFF, Jack

Dorian (1959)
   *Canadian (loan)

SITT, Hans (1850-1922)

Album Leaves, Op. 39
   *International
   *Peters (1891)
Concerto in a, Op. 68
   Eulenburg
Fantasiestücke (3), Op. 58
   Eulenburg (1894)
Gavotte and Mazurka, Op. 132
   Steingräber (1919)
Konzertstück in g, Op. 46 [orig: vla, orch]
   *Eulenburg
   *International
Konzertstück, Op. 119 [orig: vln, pno]
   Hofmeister (1916)
Morceaux (3), Op. 75
   Bosworth (1901)

SKÖLD, Yngve (1899-)

Adagio patetico
   Svenska

SKORZENY, Fritz (1900-1965)

Sonata (1952)
*Doblinger (1959)

SKRĪABIN, Aleksandr Nikolaevich (1872-1915)

Etude in c-sharp, Op. 2, No. 1 [vla, pno, or vln, pno, or vlc, pno;
   orig: pno]
   *Schirmer (Krane)
Prelude in c-sharp, Op. 9, No. 1 [orig: pno left hand]
   Günther
   *International (Borisovsky)
   *Spratt (Krane)

SLADEK, Paul (1896-)

Elegy from an Old Sketch Book [vla, pno or vln, pno]
   *Volkwein (1957)
Fantasy
   *Volkwein (1968)

SLONIMSKY, Sergey Michailovich (1932-)

Suite
   *Peters

SMITH, Julia Frances (1911-)

Pieces (2)
   *Mowbray (Doktor)

SMITH, Leland (1925-)

Sonata [vla, pno or heckelphone, pno]
   *AmCompAll

SOLARES-ECHEVARRIA, Enrique (1910-)

Ricercare sobre el nombre B-A-C-H (1941)
Ms

SOLLBERGER, Harvey (1938-)

Composition
*McGinnis

SOMERVILLE, Horace

Concerto in One Movement
Ms

SOPRONI, József (1930-)

Concerto
*Budapest
Sonatina
*Budapest

SOSEN, Otto E. von. *See* **Ebel von Sosen, Otto**

SOUKUP, Vladimír (1930-)

Sonata
*Panton

SOULAGE, Marcelle Fanny Henriette (1894-)

Sonata, Op. 25 (1926)
Buffet

SOWERBY, Leo (1895-1968)

Poem [vla, org]
Gray

Sonata (1938) [orig: clar, pno]
Schirmer (1944)

SPANNAGEL, Carl

Concerto
*Sikorski

SPEZZAFERRI, Laszlò (1912-)

Sonata in Three Tempi: Le Chant du monde (1959)
Ms

SPIES, Claudio (1925-)

Viopacem (1965)
*Boosey

SPIES, Leo (1899-1965)

Sommerbilder (5) (1954)
*Breitkopf (1955)

SPIREA, Andrei (1932-)

Symphonie de chambre [orig: vla, orch]
*IsMusPub

SPOHR, Ludwig (1784-1859)

Adagio, from *Concerto No. 7*, Op. 38 [orig: vln, orch]
Kahnt (Hermann)

SPRONGL, Norbert (1892-)

Pieces (4)
Ms

Sonata, Op. 115
  *Doblinger (1958)

SQUIRE, William Henry (1871-)
  Gavotte humoristique [orig: vlc, pno]
    Augener (1890)

STAMITZ, Anton (1754-1809)
  Concerto in B-flat
    *Schott (Lebermann/May) (1972)
  Concerto No. 2 in F
    *Schott (Lebermann/May)
  Concerto No. 3 in G
    *Breitkopf (Lebermann/Haverkampf) (1971)
  Concerto No. 4 in D
    *Bärenreiter (Lebermann/Haverkampf) (1973)
    *Breitkopf

STAMITZ, Johann Wenzel Anton (1717-1757)
  Concerto in G [orig: fl, orch; adapted for vla, 18th c.]
    *Peters (Laugg) (1962)
  Sonata in e, Op. 6a [orig: vln, b.c.]
    *International (Borisovsky)

STAMITZ, Karl (1745-1801)
  Concerto No. 1 in D, Op. 1
    *Breitkopf (Klengel) (1932)
    *International (Meyer)
    *Peters
  Concerto No. 2 in D
    Hofmeister (Borisovsky/Matz) (1960)
  Sonata in B-flat
    *International (Primrose)
    *Schott (Lebermann)
    *Vieweg (Lenzewski) (1926)

Sonata in E
International (Borisovsky)

STANFORD, Sir Charles Villiers (1852-1924)

Sonata, Op. 129 (1911) [vla, pno or clar, pno]
*Stainer (1918)

STANISLAV, Josef (1897-1971)

Sonata
Ms

STANKIEWICZ, V.

Barcarole
pub by comp (1910)

STARER, Robert (1924-)

Concerto (1958)
*MCA
Fantasy on Jewish Themes (1946)
Ms

STEFFEN, Wolfgang Johann Eberhard (1923-)

Diagramm
*Sirius

STEIN, Richard Heinrich (1882-1942)

Fantasiestücke (2) *in g* and *F*, Op. 27
Hymnophon (1909)

STEINER, Hugo von (1862- ?)

Concerto in d, Op. 43
*International (Vieland)

Concerto, Op. 44
Universal
Concerto No. 3 in a, Op. 51
Cranz (1924)
Sonata in c, Op. 53
Cranz (1926)

STEINKAULER, Walter (1873-   )

Gefundenes Glück, Op. 3, No. 1 [orig: fl, pno]
Hille

STEPANOV, Lev Borisovich (1908-   )

Miniatures (3), from *Children's Suite*
*MezhdKniga
Sonata in d (1935)
*MezhdKniga
Musgis (1959)
RussSt

STEPANOV, V.

Poem
*MezhdKniga

STEUP, H. C.

Sonata, Op. 11 [orig: hn, pno]
Steup (1819)

STEVENS, Halsey (1908-   )

Hungarian Folk Songs (3) [vla, pno or clar, pno or Eng hn, pno or vlc, pno]
*Highgate
Serenade [vla, pno or clar, pno]
*Helios

Sonata
  *AmCompAll
Suite [vla, pno or clar, pno]
  *Peer-Southern
  *Peters

STEVENS, James (1928-   )

Four Movements and a Coda
  *Moderne (1960)

STEWART, Robert J. (1918-   )

Short Pieces (3)
  *AmCompAll

STILL, Robert (1917-   )

Sonata No. 2
  *Chester (1956)

STOCKHAUSEN, Karlheinz (1928-   )

From the 7 Days
  *Universal
Plus Minus
  *Universal

STOJANOVITS, Peter Lazar (1877-1957)

Sonata in C, Op. 97
  Ms

STOJOWSKI, Sigismund (1869-1946)

Fantasia [vla, pno or trb, pno]
  Polnischer (1953)
  *PolWydMuz (Szaleski)

STOLIPIN, Ark

Lieder ohne Worte (2), Op. 28 and 29
Hofmeister (1863)

STOLZ, Ewald

Abendlied
Benjamin (1884)

STRATTON, George (1897-1954)

Concerto pastorale (1959)
*Novello

STREABBOG, L.

Waves at Play
*Belwin-Mills (Applebaum)

STRENS, Jules de (1892-   )

Sonata, Op. 54
*Belgian

STROM, Kurt Richard (1903-   )

Sonata
Ms

STRUBE, Gustav (1867-1953)

Sonata in e
Schirmer (1925)

STÜRMER, Bruno (1892-1958)

Kleine Hausmusik (1937)
*Schott (1938)

Sonata, Op. 73 [vla, pno or clar, pno]
 Müller (1957)
 *Süddeutscher

STUTSCHEVSKY, Joachim Yehoyakin (1891-)

Andante religioso
 *OR-TAV
Kol Nidrei
 *OR-TAV

SUBOTNIK, Morton (1933-)

Sonata
 *McGinnis (r)

SUCHÝ, František

Vintner's Suite [orig: vla, orch]
 *Artia

SVENDSEN, Johan (1840-1911)

Andante funèbre
 Hansen
Concerto in D, Op. 7 [orig: vlc, orch]
 Kistner (Gentz) (1905)
Romance, Op. 26 [orig: vln, orch]
 *Hansen
 Schott (Dessauer)

SVETLANOV, Evgeny Fedorovitch (1928-)

Aria
 Ms

SWAIN, Freda Mary (1902-)

Summer Rhapsody (1936)
 Ms

SWANSON, William
  Caprice
    Williams
  Elegy
    Ms

SYDEMAN, William (1928-)
  Duo [vla, hpscd or vla, pno]
    *Seesaw

SZABÓ, Ferenc (1902-1969)
  Air
    *Budapest
    Zenemükiado (1954)

SZÉKELY, Endre (1912-)
  Rhapsody No. 1
    *Budapest

SZEREMI, Gustav
  Concerto No. 1 in F, Op. 6
    Roznyai
  Concerto No. 2 in B-flat, Op. 57
    Roznyai
  Morceaux (3), Op. 33
    Roznyai (1910)

TÄGLICHSBECK, Thomas (1799-1867)
  Concertstück in C, Op. 49
    André (1867)

TAL, Joseph (1910-)
  Concerto
    *IsMusPub

Duo
   *IsMusInst
Sonata
   *IsMusPub

TANEJEW, Alexander Sergejewitsch (1850-1918)
   Album Leaf, Op. 33
      *MezhdKniga
   Feuillet d'album, Op. 38
      Jurgenson (1907)

TANSMAN, Alexander (1897-   )
   Concerto (1936)
      *Eschig

TARTINI, Giuseppe (1692-1770)
   Adagio, from *Sonata in d* [orig: vln, b.c.]
      Peters (Klengel)
   Adagio and Fugue
      *Chester (Radmall)
   Concerto in D [orig: vln, orch]
      *Eschig (Vieux)
   Sarabanda
      Schott (Moffat)
   Sonata in D [orig: vln, b.c.]
      *International (Hermann)
   Sonata in c, Op. 1, No. 10 [orig: vln, b.c.]
      *Oxford (Forbes/Richardson) (1954)
   Sonata No. 2 in F [orig: vln, b.c.]
      *International (Alard/Dessauer)

TAUSINGER, Jan (1921-   )
   Partita
      *Panton

TAUTENHAHN, Gunther

Sonata (1969)
  *Seesaw

TAVARES, Mario (1928-   )

Balada (1945) [vla, pno or vlc, pno]
  Ms

TCHAIKOVSKY, Peter Illytch. *See* Chaĭkovskiĭ, Petr Il'ich

TELEMANN, Georg Philipp (1681-1767)

Concerto in G
  *Amadeus (Beyer) (1974)
  *Bärenreiter (Füssl)
  *ElkanH (Courte)
  *International (Katims)
Sonata in a [orig: vl da gamba, b.c.]
  *International (Shulz/Vieland)
  *Peters
  *Schott (Dolmetsch/Wood)
Sonata in B-flat [vla, b.c.]
  *Schott (Ruf)
Sonata in D
  *International (Upmeyer/Vieland)
Sonata in D
  *Broekmans (Leerink)
Sonata in e, from *Essercizii Musici* [vla, pno or vl da gamba, pno or vlc, pno; orig: vl da gamba, b.c.]
  *Peters (Rubardt)
Sonata in G, from *Der getreue Musikmeister* [vla, b.c. or vl da gamba, b.c.]
  *Bärenreiter (Längin)
Suite in D [orig: vla, str orch]
  *Schott (Bergmann/Forbes) (1952)
  Schirmer

TERIAN, M.

Suite (1930)
Ms

TERTIS, Lionel (1876-)

Blackbirds
Schott
Hier au soir: Pensee musical
Schott (1925)
Old Irish Air
*Schott
Romance
Schott (1923)
Sunset: Coucher de soleil
Chester (1923)
Tune
Augener

THERON, J.

Pieces (2)
Hamelle (ca. 1890)

THERSTAPPEN, Hans Joachim (1905-)

Kammersonate, Op. 11 (1929)
Ms

THILMAN, Johannes Paul (1906-1973)

Sonata in c-sharp (1935)
Ms

THOMAS, Ambroise (1811-1896)

Gavotte, from *Mignon* [orig: orch]
*Fischer (Isaac/Lewis)

THOMAS, Anton

Morceaux de salon, Op. 5
Universal (1885)

THOMAS, E.

Sonatina in C
Augener

THURNER, E.

Sonata, Op. 29 [orig: hn, pno]
Peters (1817)

TICCIATI, Niso (1924-1972)

Ballad and Moto perpetuo, from *Suite* [orig: vla, chamb orch]
*Oxford
Minuet and Berceuse
*Oxford (Copperwheat)
Musette, Polka melancolique, and *Galop*, from *Suite* [orig: vla, chamb orch]
*Oxford
Prelude, Carol, and *Christmas Dance*, from *Suite* [orig: vla, chamb orch]
*Oxford
Scherzo and Toccata
*Oxford (Copperwheat)

TIESSEN, Heinz (1887-1971)

Music, Op. 59 [vla, org]
*Ries&Erler
Serious Melodies (2), Op. 29, No. 2b and Op. 30, No. 2b
*Ries&Erler (1948)

TILLIS, Frederick C.

Phantasy and Allegro
*AmCompAll

TISBE, Henri

Albumblatt in g, Op. 7
    Breitkopf (1887)
Serenade in g
    Cranz (1884)

TLIL, Amali

Concerto
    *Jobert

TOCH, Ernst (1887-1964)

Impromptus (3), Op. 90
    *Belwin-Mills

TOLDRÁ, Eduardo (1895-1962)

Dels quatre vents, from *Seis sonetos* [orig: vln, pno]
    *UnMusEsp (Amaz)
La Font, from *Seis sonetos* [orig: vln, pno]
    *UnMusEsp (Amaz)
Oracio al maig, from *Seis sonetos* [orig: vln, pno]
    *UnMusEsp (Amaz)
Soneti de la rosada, from *Seis sonetos* [orig: vln, pno]
    *UnMusEsp (Amaz)

TOMASI, Henri-Frédien (1901-1971)

Concerto
    *Leduc

TOMC, Matija (1899-)

Caprice
    *Društva
Elegija
    *Društva

TORANDELL, A.

Sonata, Op. 21
   Deiss (1921)

TOVEY, Sir Donald Francis (1875-1940)

Sonata in B-flat, Op. 16 (1912)
   Schott (1912)

TRADITIONAL

French Air (18th century)
   Schott (Tertis/Burmester)
Home on the Range
   *Kjos (Buchtel)
Londonderry Air
   *Fischer (Ambrosio/Isaac/Lewis)
   *Schott(London) (Tertis)
   *Volkwein (Primrose/Spalding)
Old McDonald in the Dell
   *Kjos (Buchtel)
Turn Ye to Me (Scottish Song)
   Oxford (Moore) (1949)
When Love is Kind
   *Kjos (Buchtel)

TRANTOW, Herbert Otto Karl (1903-   )

Duo (1936)
   *Mitteldeutscher (1951)
   Peters (1950)

TREMBLAY, George Amédée (1911-   )

For Viola and Piano
   *AmCompAll

TREVANI, Francesco

Sonata No. 1 in E-flat
  *Doblinger (Stierhof)
  Ricordi
Sonata No. 2 in c
  *Doblinger (Stierhof)
  Ricordi
Sonata No. 3 in B-flat
  *Doblinger (Stierhof)
  Ricordi
Sonatas (9) [vla, hpscd]
  Ms

TREXLER, Georg (1903-)

Sonatina (1953)
  *Breitkopf (1954)

TRIMBLE, Lester (1923-)

Duo (1949)
  Ms

TROMMER, A.

Hungarian Serenade, Op. 380 [orig: vlc, pno]
  Breitkopf (Hermann) (1898)

TSCHEMBERDSCHY, N

Suite, Op. 4 (1932)
  Leeds
  RussSt (1932)
  Universal

TSCHIRSCH, Heinrich Julius (1820- ?)

Impromptu-Solo, Op. 69
  Pohl (1868)

TSINTSADZE, Sulkhan Fedorovich (1925-   )
Chorumi: Grusinischer Tanz
Musgis (1950)

TÜMLER, Rudolf
Elegy: "Was ist das Glück," Op. 11
Gleis (1937)

TÜRCKE, Karl
Theme and Variations, Op. 9 [orig: vla, org]
Kahnt (1891)

TURINA, Joaquín (1882-1949)
Andante
RussSt (1958)

TUTHILL, Burnet Corwin (1888-   )
Sonata, Op. 20
*SouthernTX (1969)

TWEEDY, Donald (1890-   )
Sonata (1916)
Ms

TZITOVICH, V.
Triptych
*MezhdKniga

URIBE-HOLGUÍN, Guillermo (1880-   )
Sonata, Op. 24
Ms

VALENSIN, Georges

> *Minuet*
> *International (Katims)

VALENTINI, Giuseppe (ca. 1681-ca. 1740)

> *Sonata No. 10 in E* [orig: vln, b.c.]
> *PolWydMuz (Rakowski/Jahnke)

VALLE, [?]

> *Ao pe da fogueira* (*Preludio XV*)
> *Fischer (Heifetz/Primrose)

VALLENTIN, Artur (1906-)

> *Sonata*, Op. 37
> pub by comp (1942)

VAN DE VATE, Nancy (1931-)

> *Sonata*
> *Tritone

VAN DOREN, Theo

> *Exaltation*, Op. 14
> Maurer (1959)

VAŇHAL, Jan Křtitel (Johann Baptist) (1732-1813)

> *Concertino in F* [orig: vla, orch]
> *Doblinger (Weinmann)
> *Concerto in C*
> *Artia (Blažek/Plichta)
> *International

Sonata, Op. 7
   Stainer (ca. 1916)
Sonata in E-flat
   *Doblinger (Weinmann) (1973)
   *Wollenweber

VARDI, Emanuel (1915-)
   Suite on American Folk Songs [orig: vla, orch]
      Schirmer (1950)

VARGAS-WALLIS, Darwin (1925-)
   Sonata No. 1 (1963-1968)
      Ms

VASSILENKO, Sergei Nikiforovich (1872-1956)
   Sonata, Op. 46
      *MezhdKniga

VAUCORBEIL, Auguste-Emmanuel (1821-1884)
   Grande sonate in A
      Heugel (1862)

VAUGHAN WILLIAMS, Ralph (1872-1958)
   Fantasia on *"Greensleeves"* [orig: orch]
      MusUn
      *Oxford (Forbes)
   Romance [orig: harmonica, orch]
      *Oxford
   Studies in English Folk Song (6)
      *Stainer
   Suite [orig: vla, orch]
      Oxford (Douglas)

VEPRIK, Alexander Moiseyevitch (1899-   )

Rhapsody, Op. 11
  *MezhdKniga

VERACINI, Francesco Maria (1690-ca. 1750)

Largo
   International (Katims)
Sonata in e   [orig: vln, b.c.]
   Boosey
   *International

VERHEY, Th. H. H.

Character Pieces (4), Op. 3 [orig: clar, pno]
   Leuckart (1873)

VERRALL, John W. (1908-   )

Concerto
   *AmCompAll
Sonata No. 1
   *AmCompAll
   Peters (1956)
Sonata No. 2
   *Peters
Sonatina
   *AmCompAll

VERSTOVSKY, Alexey Nicolayevitch (1799-1862)

Variations on Two Themes
   *MezhdKniga (Borisovsky)

VIERNE, Louis (1870-1937)

Legende
   Leduc

Le Soir
Leduc

VIEUX, Maurice Edgard (1884-   )

Etude de concert No. 1 in C
  *Eschig
Etude de concert No. 2 in b
  *Eschig
Etude de concert No. 3 in G
  *Eschig
Etude de concert No. 4 in f
  *Eschig
Etude de concert No. 5 in c-sharp
  *Eschig
Etude de concert No. 6 in f-sharp
  *Eschig
Pieces (2): *Scherzo and Etude de concert No. 2*
  *Leduc (1926)
Scherzo [vla, pno or vlc, pno]
  Leduc (1928)

VIEUXTEMPS, Henri (1820-1881)

Allegro and Scherzo in B-flat, from an *Unfinished Sonata*
  Jobert (1884)
Elegy, Op. 30
  André (1954)
  Augener (1898)
  Litolff (1912)
  *Sikorski (Schmidtner)
Romance, Op. 40, No. 1
  Schott
Sonata in B-flat, Op. 36
  *Amadeus (Beyer) (1974)
  Peters (1863)

VIGUERIE, Bernard (1761-1819)

Sonatine in C
  *Belwin-Mills (Applebaum)

VIGUIER, A.

Fantaisie, Op. 3
Costallat (ca. 1860)
Morceaux de salon, Op. 1
Costallat (ca. 1860)
Rêverie, Op. 7; *Andante and Allegretto*
Costallat
Romance and Canzonette, Op. 4
Costallat

VILLA-LOBOS, Heitor (1887-1959)

Aria, from *Bachianas Brasileiras No. 5* [orig: voice, 8 vlc]
*Associated (Primrose)

VITACEK, Fabian

Theme and Variations, Op. 7
Ms

VITALI, Tomaso Antonio (1663-1745)

Chaconne in g [orig: vln, b.c.]
*Breitkopf (Hermann)
*Schirmer (Bailly)

VITETTA, M.

Etude No. 1
Patelson

VIVALDI, Antonio (1678-1741)

Adagio and Allegro in d
Novello (Jacob)
Concerto [orig: vla d'amore, orch]
*MezhdKniga (Borisovsky)

Concerto in d
  *Budapest
Concerto in A, F. II, No. 1 [orig: vla d'amore, orch]
  *Belwin-Mills (Townsend)
Concerto in d, Op. 3, No. 6 [orig: vln, orch]
  *Schirmer (Mogill)
Concerto in e [orig: Sonata in e for vlc and b.c., Op. 14, No. 5]
  *International (Primrose)
Concerto No. 19 in A
  *Transatlantiques (Oubradous)
Sonata in A
  *International (David/Hermann)
Sonata in A, Op. 2, No. 2
  Breitkopf
Sonata in B-flat, F. XIV, No. 6 [orig: vlc, b.c.]
  *International (Primrose)
Sonata in g, F. XIV, No. 9 [orig: vlc, b.c.]
  *International (Katims)
Sonata No. 3 in a
  *International (Primrose)
Sonatas (6), Op. 17 [orig: vlc, b.c.]
  *International (Primrose/Dallapiccola) (1955)
Suite in a [orig: vln, b.c.]
  RussSt (Sebor)
Suite in B-flat
  Costallat
Suite in E-flat
  *Leduc (R. Boulay/L. Boulay)

VOGEL, Heinrich

Morceaux (3), Op. 1
  Schott (1861)

VOLKMANN, Robert (1815-1883)

Musical Picture Book, Op. 11
  *Augener (Hermann)
Romance in E
  Breitkopf

VON KOCH, Erland. *See* Koch, Sigurd Christian Erland von

VOORMOLEN, Alexander Nicolas (1895-)

Sonata (1953)
*Donemus (1954)

VOTOČEK, Emil (1862-1950)

Ballatine (3)
  Hudebni (Černý) (1945)
Fantasy (1943)
  Ms
Suite
  Ms

VRÁNA, František (1914-)

Sonatina (1940)
  Ms

VREDENBURG, Max (1904-)

Lamento (1953)
*Donemus (1955)

VREMŠAK, Samo (1930-)

Suite
  *Društva

VREULS, Victor (1876-1944)

Poeme
  Bosworth

WAGNER, Alfred

Scherzo espagnol
    *Sirius

WAGNER, Richard (1813-1883)

Album-Leaf [orig: pno]
    *Augener
Entrance of the Black Swan, from *Lohengrin* [orig: orch]
    Suvini-Zerboni (Polo)
Song to the Evening Star, from *Tannhäuser* [orig: voice, orch]
    *Fischer (Isaac/Lewis)
Träume (*Wesendonck Lieder, No. 5*) [orig: voice, pno]
    *Schott (Primrose)

WALCKIERS, Eugène

Sonata in E-flat, Op. 91 [orig: vln, pno]
    Costallat

WALKER, Ernest (1870-1949)

Romance in B-flat, Op. 9
    MusUn
    Williams
Sonata in C, Op. 29
    Schott (1912)
Variations on an Original Theme
    MusUn
    *Novello (1953)

WALLACE, William

Sonata
    *Canadian (loan)

WALLNER, Leopold

Berceuse in A-flat
    Schott (1909)

Rhapsody
  Schott (1909)
Suite polonaise
  Schott (1896)

WALTHEW, Richard Henry (1872-1951)

Mediations (4) [vla, pno or clar, pno]
  Boosey
A Mosaic in 10 Pieces [vla, pno or clar, pno]
  Boosey
Regret and Conversation galante
  *Boosey
Serenade-Sonata in F
  Williams (1925)
Suite in F [orig: clar, pno]
  Boosey

WALTON, Sir William Turner (1902-)

The Call of the Angelus
  Boosey
Concerto (rev. 1962)
  *Oxford
Sonata (1938) [spurious]
  Oxford

WALZEL, Leopold Matthias (1902-)

Sonata ariosa, Op. 30 (1960)
  *Doblinger (1961)

WANHAL, Johann Baptist. *See* **Vaňhal, Jan Křtitel**

WARD, Robert E. (1917-)

Arioso and Tarantelle (1954) [vla, pno or vlc, pno]
  *Highgate

WARNER, Harry Waldo (1874-1945)

A Valse Caprice, Op. 20, No. 6
Fischer

WARREN, Elinor Remick (1905-)

Poem
Fischer

WASSILENKO, Sergei N. (1872-)

Sonata in g, Op. 46 (1923)
Leeds
Musgis (1955)
Suite aus Stücken des 17 Jahrhunderts (*Zodiacus musicus* von J. A.
Schmierer)
Ms

WATSON, Walter

Lyric Piece
*Ludwig

WEBBER, Andrew Lloyd

Sonatina
*Augener

WEBER, Ben (1916-)

Chorale and Variations, Op. 18 (1943)
Ms

WEBER, Friedrich Dionys (1766- ?)

Duos faciles et recreatifs (6), Op. 18
Schott (1890)

WEBER, Karl Maria Friedrich Ernst, Freiherr von (1786-1826)
Air, from *Der Freischütz* [orig: voice, orch]
   Augener (Kreuz)
Andante and Rondo ongarese in c, Op. 35 [orig: bsn, orch]
   *International (Primrose) (1956)
   *Schott (Schünemann)
Grand duo concertant in E-flat, Op. 48 [orig: clar, pno]
   Lienau (1881)
Serenata, from *Petites pièces faciles*, Op. 3, No. 1 [orig: pno 4 hands]
   *Schott (Forbes) (1958)
Variations on the Folksong "A Schusserl und a Reind'rl" (1806)
   Morawe (1927)

WEICKMANN, A.
Gebet
   Rahter (1892)
Nachtlied, Op. 4, No. 1
   Rahter (1890)

WEILLER, E.
Au pied de la croix: Adagio [orig: vln, pno]
   Durand (1926)
Malaguena: Danse espagnole
   Enoch
Prière, Op. 280
   Enoch
Rêve
   Enoch
Souffrance
   Enoch

WEINER, Laslo (1885-)
Ballade, Op. 18 (1912)
   Kultura
Sonata (1939)
   Zenemükiado (1961)

Werbungstanz aus Pereg, Op. 40
Zenemükiado (1953)

WEINER, Leo (1885-1960)
Ballade, Op. 8 [vla, pno or clar, pno]
Rozsavölgyi
Sonata, Op. 9
*Budapest (Lukács)

WEISS, Ferdinand (1933-   )
Sonata (1958)
Ms

WEISSENBORN, Ernst
Im hellen Mondschein, Op. 200
SchmidtCF
In der Dämmerung, Op. 194 [orig: vln, pno]
SchmidtCF
Lied ohne Worte, Op. 226 [orig: vln, pno]
SchmidtCF
Romance, Op. 227
SchmidtCF

WEIST-HILL, Thomas Henry (1823-1891)
Romance and Slumber Song
Williams (1902)

WELANDER, Waldemar (1899-   )
Sonatina
Breitkopf

WENNER, Emile
Chanson d'avril, Op. 22 [orig: vln, str quin]
Costallat

Nocturne, Op. 16 [orig: vln, pno]
Costallat
Pieces (2), Op. 13
Costallat (ca. 1880)

WEPRIK, Alexander (1899-1958)

Rhapsody, Op. 11
RussSt (1929)
Universal
Totenlieder (4), Op. 4
Jüdische (1925)

WERMANN, Friedrich Oskar (1840-1906)

Vortragsstücke (2), Op. 61
Hug (1893)

WESTERMANN, Helmut (1895-)

Konzertante Musik, Op. 34 [orig: vla, str orch]
*SimBenjRaht

WEYRAUCH, Johannes (1897-)

Herzliebster Jesu (*Passion Sonata*) (1932) [vla, org]
*Hänssler

WHETTAM, Graham

Concerto, Op. 16
deWolfe

WHITTENBERG, Charles (1927-)

Set for Two (1962)
AmCompAll

WIDOR, Charles Marie (1845-1937)

Andante, from *Organ Symphony No. 8* [orig: org]
  Hamelle (van Waefelghem)

WIENIAWSKI, Henryk (1835-1880)

Caprices (2), Op. 10, No. 5 and Op. 18. No. 4 [orig: vln]
  *Hinrichsen (Forbes)
Reverie in f-sharp
  Rahter (1890)

WIERNSBERGER, J. A.

Cantilene melancolique
  Lemoine (1890)
Cantilene pastorale
  Lemoine (1890)

WIGGLESWORTH, Frank (1918-)

Sound Piece
  *AmCompAll

WIHTOL, Joseph (1863-1948)

Recitative, Op. 14
  Belaieff (1894)

WILHELMJ, August Emil Daniel Ferdinand Viktor (1845-1908)

Romance in E, Op. 10
  Lienau
  Schlesinger (Dessauer)

WILSON, George Balch (1927-)

Sonata
  *Jobert (1969)

WINKLER, Alexander Adolfowitsch (1865-1935)

Meditation élégiaque, Op. 31, No. 1
 Belaieff
Morceaux (2), Op. 31
 Belaieff (1935)
Sonata in C, Op. 10 (1902)
 Belaieff
 *MezhdKniga
 Musgis (1955)
La Toupie, Op. 31, No. 2
 Belaieff

WITNI, Monica (1928-)

Concerto in c
 Ms

WITTENBECHER, Otto (1875-)

Cradle Song (*Berceuse*), Op. 19
 Rahter
Liebeslied, Op. 7
 Forberg (1904)

WITTMANN, Robert

Barcarole, Op. 50
 Hofmeister (1874)

WOLPERT, Franz Alfons (1917-)

Ritornell
 Heinrichshofen (1954)

WOLSTENHOLME, William (1865-1931)

Allegretto
 Novello (1900)

Canzona
    *Novello (Tertis)
Romance in B-flat
    *Novello (1900)

WOOD, Hugh (1932-)

Variations (1958)
    *Universal (Aronowitz) (1960)

WOOD, Joseph (1915-)

Sonata
    *AmCompAll

WORDSWORTH, William Brockelsby (1908-)

Intermezzo, Op. 2b (1934)
    Ms

WORK, Henry Clay (1832-1884)

Grandfather's Clock [orig: voice, pno]
    *Belwin-Mills (Applebaum)

WRAY, John

Capriccioso
    Oxford (1947)
A Simple Suite
    Oxford

WUENSCH, Gerhard J. (1925-)

Sonatina, Op. 15
    *Canadian (loan)

WUNDERER, Alexander (1877-1955)

> *Sonata*, Op. 21 (1946)
> *Doblinger (1953)

WUSTROW, A. F.

> *Duo in B-flat*, Op. 7
> Peters (1828)

WYMAN, Dann

> *Sonata*
> *Seesaw

WYNNE, David (1900-)

> *Sonata* (1951)
> Ms
> *Sonatina* (1946)
> Ms

YANNATOS, James (1929-)

> *Fantasy*
> *AmCompAll

YUILLE-SMITH, C. R.

> *Romance*
> Oxford (1932)

YVON, C.

> *Sonata in F* [orig: Eng hn, pno]
> Ricordi

ZAFRED, Mario (1922-)
Concerto
  *Ricordi
Elegy [orig: vla, orch]
  *Ricordi

ZAMACOIS, Joaquin (1894-)
Serenada d'hivern
  *UnMusEsp (Amaz)

ZEIDMAN, Boris Isaacovich (1908-)
Concertino
  *MCA (1972)
Concerto No. 2
  *MezhdKniga

ZEISL, S.
Sonata in a (1950)
  *Doblinger (Reher) (1955)

ZELINKA, Jan Evangelista (1893-)
Fantasy
  Ms

ZELTER, Carl Friedrich (1758-1832)
Concerto in E-flat
  Breitkopf (1785-1787)
  *Grahl

ZICH, Otakar (1879-1934)
Elegy
  *Artia

ZINZADSE, Sulchan. *See* Tsintsadze, Sulkhan Fedorovich

ZITTERBART, F. Jr.

Barcarole in g, and *Lied ohne Worte*
Church (1897)

ZOLOTAREV, Vassily Andreyevitch (1873-)

Eclogue, Op. 38
RussSt (ca. 1920)

ZRNO, Felix (1890-)

Sonatina
Ms
Suite, Op. 60 (1946)
Ms
Variace na Lid. Pis. Moravskou
Ms

ZUCKERT, León (1904-)

Short Suite (*Suite Corta*) (1974) [vla, pno or trp, pno or clar, pno]
*Canadian (loan)

ZUR LINDE, Karl

Piece (1929)
Ms

Anthologies

Album of Favorite Pieces in First Position
Presser

BERGER, [?] , ed.

Viola Solos for Study and Performance
*MCA

BOETJI, J., ed,

Viola Music for Concert and Church
Boston

BRECK, E. S., ed.

Christmas Joys
*Fischer

BRODSZKY, Ferenc, ed.

Old Music for Viola
*Budapest

CATHEART, [?] , ed.

Solo Album for Viola
Boosey

CLASSENS, [?] , ed.

Alto classique, 2 vols.
*Philippo

CONUS, Jules; KATIMS, Milton; and BORISOVSKY, Vadim, eds.

Album of Six Pieces
*International

DODD, Raymond H., ed.

Viola-Album
*Schott

DOKTOR, Paul, ed.

First Solos for the Viola Player
*Schirmer
Solos for the Viola Player
*Schirmer

Easy Viola Solos
*Consolidated

ERRANTE, Belisario, ed.

Viola Player's Solo Album
*Shawnee

ETLING, Forest R., ed.

Solo Time for Strings, 4 vols.
*Etling (1965-1970)

FLETCHER, Stanley; ROLLAND, Paul; ROWELL, Margaret; and KROLICK, Edward, eds.

New Tunes for Strings, 2 vols.
*Boosey

FORBES, Watson, ed.

A Book of Classical Pieces, 2 vols.
*Oxford
Classical and Romantic Pieces for Viola and Piano
*Oxford (1974)
A First Year Classical Album
*Oxford
A Second Year Classical Album
*Oxford

FORBES, Watson, and **RICHARDSON**, Alan, eds.

Scottish Tunes
Oxford

HANIZKI, Th. v., ed.

Klassisches und Modernes
Challier (1886)

HARVEY, Harold Ryder, ed.

The Viola Player's Repertory
Ditson

HERFURTH, C. Paul, ed.

Classical Album of Early Grade Pieces
*Boston

HERFURTH, C. Paul, and **DEVERITCH**, [?], eds.

Viola and Piano Music
*Willis

HERMANN, Friedrich, ed.

Album, 2 vols.
*Augener

HRUBY, Frank, ed.

Hruby Viola Folio: 1st to 3rd Position Solos
*Brook

ISAAC, Merle J., ed.

Sacred Music
*Fischer

Der Kleine Soloist
> Seeling (1888)

KLENGEL, Paul, ed.

Album of 24 Classical Pieces, 3 vols.
> *International
> *Peters (1932)

Altitalienische Gesänge
> Simrock (1923)

Viola Album (9 Pieces from the 3 Volumes of Classic Pieces)
> *Peters

Vortrags-Album, 2 vols.
> Breitkopf (1920, 1922)

KREUZ, Emil, ed.

25 Pieces
> Augener (1896)

KRITCH, [?], ed.

First Book of Viola Pieces
> Witmark

LAUBACH, Alfred, ed.

Album classique
> Augener (1903)

McCALL, Harlo E., ed.

Instrumental Hymn Favorites
> *Fischer

MEYER, Clemens, ed.

Alte Meister des Violaspiels, 2 vols.
> Peters (1953)
> Rieter (1900) (6 vols.)

MOFFAT, Alfred, ed.

Old Masters for Young Players
Associated

MOFFAT, Alfred, and LAUBACH, Alfred, eds.

Album classique, 2 vols.
Augener (1903)
Schott

MURRAY, [?], and BROWN, [?], eds.

Tunes for My Viola
*Boosey

MURRAY, Eleanor, and TATE, Phyllis, eds.

The New Viola Books, 3 vols.
*Oxford
Tunes Old and New
*Oxford

Old Masters of the Viola

*Peters

PALASCHKO, Johannes, ed.

Alte Meister für Junge Spieler
*Schott

RADMALL, Peggy, ed.

The Chesterian Viola Series, 2 vols.
*Chester

REITIKH, [?], ed.

Anthology of Teaching Repertoire, 2 vols.
*MezhdKniga

Etudes and Virtuoso Pieces
  *MezhdKniga
Pieces (5) *by Russian and Soviet Composers*
  *MezhdKniga

RITTER, Hermann, ed.

  Bunte Reihe
    Simon (1896)
  Miszellen, Sammlung von Vortragsstücken verschiedener Tondichter, 2 vols.
    Vieweg (1904)
  Musikalische Juwelen
    Rühle (1894)
  Repertorium
    Schmid (1878)
  Übertragungen
    Kistner (1885)

ROBERTSON, Leroy J., ed.

  Hymns from the Crossroads
    *Fischer

ROOD, Louise, ed.

  Old Dances for Young Violas (*1st Position*)
    *McGinnis

SITT, Hans, ed.

  Sammlung, 2 vols.
    Steingräber (1919)

Solo Album for Viola
    Boosey

STEHLING, K. A., ed.

  Album
    *Augener

String Americana, 2 vols.

Harms

SZALESKI, [?], ed.

Works by Polish Composers
*PolWydMuz

TATALIAN, [?], ed.

Pieces (4) by Soviet Composers
*MezhdKniga
Works by Soviet Composers
*MezhdKniga

Ten Easy Solos

Heacox

34 Viola Solos with Piano Accompaniment
*Belwin-Mills

Viola Miniatures (A Collection of 9 Solos)
*Fischer

WALTON, [?], ed.

Solo Album for Viola
Boosey

WHISTLER, Harvey S., ed.

Concert and Contest Collection (Third Position)
*Rubank
Solos for Strings
*Rubank

VIOLA WITH NON-KEYBOARD

BAX, Arnold Edward Trevor (1883-1953)

Fantasy Sonata [vla, harp]
Murdoch

BEETHOVEN, Ludwig van (1770-1827)

Allegro [vla, guit]
*Zimmermann (Schmidt) (1970)

HEINISCH, Victor

Traumerei, Op. 30 [vla, harp]
Simon

LAUFFENSTEINER, Wolff Jakob

Duetto in A [vla, guit]
*Doblinger (Schaller)

MAMLOK, Ursula

Music [vla, harp]
*AmCompAll

MARCELLO, Benedetto (1686-1739)

Sonata in G [vla, guit or vla, lute; orig: vl da gamba]
*Zimmermann (Azpiazu)

PAGANINI, Niccolò (1782-1840)

Sonata "per la grande viola" [vla, guit]
Ms

PARCHMAN, Gene Louis (1929-   )

Sonata [vla, perc]
*Seesaw

PORTER, Quincy (1897-1966)

Duo (1957) [vla, harp or vla, hpscd]
Associated

SCHICKELE, Peter (1935-   )

Windows: 3 Pieces [vla, guit]
*Tetra

SCHWARTZ, Elliott Shelling (1936-   )

Aria No. 3 (1967) [vla, woodblocks]
*Fischer (1972)

TELEMANN, Georg Philipp (1681-1767)

Sonata in a [vla, guit or vla, lute; orig: vl da gamba]
*Zimmermann (Azpiazu)

WASHBURN, Gary

Zeitdehner
*Seesaw

VIOLA WITH ELECTRONICS

BIGGS, John (1932-)
Invention (1972) [vla, tape]
Ms

FRITSCH, Johannes G. (1941-)
Partita [vla, contact microphone, magnetophone, filter, Regler Band]
*Moderne

HANNAY, Roger
Elegy [vla, tape]
*Media

IVEY, Jean Eichelberger (1923-)
Aldebaran [vla, tape]
*Fischer (1974)

LAZAROF, Henri (1932-)
Cadence II (*Cadence for Milton*) (1969) [vla, tape]
*Bote&Bock (1971)

STOCKHAUSEN, Karlheinz (1928-)
Solo (1965-1966) [melody inst, feedback]
*Universal

Spiral [1 player, short-wave radio]
*Universal

SUBOTNIK, Morton (1933-)

Mandolin [vla, tape, film]
*MCA (r)

VIOLA WITH CHAMBER ENSEMBLE

AMON, Johann (1763-1825)

Larghetto and 2 Themes varies, Op. 115 [vla, str trio]
André (1824)
Trois quatuors concertantes, Op. 15 [vla, str trio]
André (1802)

ATTERN, Wilhelm

Variations and Rondo on a Theme from "Die weisse Dame" by Boildieu
[vla, str trio]
Langewiesche (1835)

BERIO, Luciano (1925-)

Chemins II (1968) [vla, chamb ens]
*Universal (r)

BRANT, Henry Dreyfus (1913-1976)

Hieroglyphics (1957) [vla, timp, chimes, celesta, harp]
AmCompAll

CAVALLINI, Eugenio (1806- ?)

Divertimento in G [vla, str quar]
Breitkopf (1829)

COLGRASS, Michael Charles (1932-   )

Theme and Variations [vla, 4 drums]
*MusPerc

DELLO, Joio, Norman (1913-   )

Lyric Fantasies [vla, str quar or vla, str orch]
*Associated (1975)

FELDMAN, Morton (1926-   )

The Viola in My Life I [vla, chamb ens]
*Universal (r)
The Viola in My Life II [vla, chamb ens]
*Universal (r)

GERMANO, Carlo (1831-   ?)

Remembrance [vla, str quar]
Pleyel (1831)

GOEB, Roger (1914-   )

Concertant IIIb [vla, double wind quin]
*AmCompAll

HARRIS, Roy (1898-   )

Quintet (1939) [vla, str quar]
Ms

HEMSI, Alberto (1898-   )

Quintet [vla, str quar]
*Universal

KOHSER, E.

Abendglöckchen, Romance [vla, str quar]
Seeling (ca. 1890)

KRUSE, Wilhelm (1872-)

Nocturne [vla, str quar]
Oertel (ca. 1890)

MARQUE, Auguste (1773- ?)

Theme varie, Op. 51 [vla, str trio]
Gallet (ca. 1860)

MAURER, Ludwig Wilhelm (1789-1878)

Divertimento, Op. 85 [vla, str quar]
Peters (1861)

MEJO, W.

Concertino in C [vla, str quar]
Häcker (1840)

MERIGHI, Vincenzo (1795- ?)

Divertimento [vla, str quar]
Ricordi (1820)

SIEGEL, Otto (1896-)

Concertino in e, Op. 124 [vla, str quar]
Ms

VIOLA WITH ORCHESTRA

ABSIL, Jean
Concerto, Op. 54. *See* Viola with Keyboard

ADLER, Samuel H. (1928-   )
Song and Dance
   *Oxford (r)

ALBIN, Roger (1920-   )
Tre pezzi pazzi
   *Rideau (r)

ANGERER, Paul (1927-   )
Concerto (1947)
      pub by comp
Concerto (1962) [vla, chamb orch]
      *Doblinger (1971)

ANLEU-DÍAZ, Enrique (1940-   )
Concerto (1968)
      Ms

Anonymous
Concerto in D, from *V Concerti à Viola Concertato*
      Breitkopf (1762)

ANTĨUFEEV, Boris Ivanovich
Concerto, Op. 45. *See* Viola with Keyboard

ARENDS, H.
Concertino in C, Op. 7
International
*Jurgenson (1908)

ARISTAKESĨAN, Emin Aspetovich
Concerto. *See* Viola with Keyboard

ARNOLD, Malcolm Henry (1921-   )
Concerto, Op. 108
*Faber (r)

BACEWICZ, Grażyna (1913-1969)
Concerto
*PolWydMuz (r)

BACH, Carl Philipp Emanuel (1714-1788)
Frühlingserwachen [vla, str orch]
SchmidtCF (Pagels)

BACH, Johann Christian (1735-1782)
Concerto in B-flat [orig: bsn, orch]
*Billaudot (Massis) (r)
Concerto in c
*Salabert (Casadesus) (r)

BACH, Johann Sebastian (1685-1750)
Air, from *Suite No. 3 in D*, BWV 1068 [vla, str orch; orig: orch]
Benjamin (Ritter)

Arioso, from *Cantata No. 156, "Ich steh mit einem Fuss im Grabe"* [vla, str orch]
  *BroudeBr (Luck)

BADINGS, (Henk) Hendrik Herman (1907-)
  Concerto [vla, str orch]
    *Donemus (r)

BAEYENS, August Louis (1895-1966)
  Concerto, Op. 54 (1956)
    Metropolis

BAKER, Michael
  Counterplay (1973) [vla, str orch]
    *Canadian (loan)

BALLOU, Esther Williamson (1915-)
  Konzerstück
    *AmCompAll

BANCQUART, Alain (1934-)
  Concerto
    *Jobert (r)

BARGIEL, Woldemar
  Adagio, Op. 38. *See* Viola with Keyboard

BARTEL, Hans-Christian (1932-)
  Concerto
    *DeutschVerMus (r)

BARTÓK, Béla (1881-1945)
  Concerto (1945)
  *Boosey (Serly) (1949) (r)

BATE, Stanley Richard (1911-1959)
  Concerto (1946)
  *Schott (1951)

BAUR, Jürg (1918-)
  Concerto [vla, chamb orch]
  Breitkopf (1959)

BAX, Arnold Edward Trevor
  Phantasy. *See* Viola with Keyboard

BECK, Conrad Arthur
  Concerto. *See* Viola with Keyboard

BECKER, John J. (1886-1961)
  Concerto (1937)
  *AmCompAll (r)

BEKKU, Sadao (1922-)
  Concerto [vla, 2 irregular orchs]
  Ms

BENDA, Georg (1722-1795)
  Concerto No. 1 in F
  Breitkopf (1778)
  *Schott (Lebermann)
  Concerto No. 2 in E-flat
  Breitkopf (1778)

BENJAMIN, Arthur L. (1893-1960)

Sonata or Concerto. Elegy, Waltz, and *Toccata*
*Boosey (r)

BEREZOWSKY, Nicolai (1900-1953)

Concerto, Op. 28 (1941)
Boosey

BERIO, Luciano (1925-)

Chemins IIB
*Universal (r)
Chemins III (1968)
*Universal (r)

BERLIOZ, Hector (1803-1869)

Harold in Italy, Op. 16
*Eulenburg
*International
*Kalmus

BERLYN, Johann

Nocturne, Op. 161
André (1865)

BLACHER, Boris (1903-)

Concerto, Op. 48
*Bote&Bock (Lombardo) (1956)

BLANK, J.

Concerto in C, Op. 3
Hummel (ca. 1816)

BLENDINGER, Herbert

Concerto
    *Orlando (r)

BLOCH, Ernest (1880-1959)

Suite (1919-1920)
    *Schirmer (r)
Suite Hébraique (1919)
    *Schirmer (1940) (r)

BLOMDAHL, Karl-Birger (1916-1968)

Concerto (1941)
    Ms

BOTTJE, Will Gay (1925-   )

Rhapsodic Variations [vla, pno, str orch]
    *AmCompAll (r)

BOURGUIGNON, Francis de (1890-1961)

Suite, Op. 67 (1940)
    Hulpiau

BOWEN, Edwin York (1884-1961)

Concerto (1935)
    Ms

BOZAY, Attila (1939-   )

Pezzo concertato, Op. 11
    *Budapest (r)

BOZZA, Eugène Joseph (1905-)
Concertino
*Ricard (r)

BRAEIN, Edvard Fliflet (1924-)
Serenade
*Lyche (1947) (r)

BRANT, Henry Dreyfus (1913-1976)
Concerto (1940)
Ms

BRETSCHNEIDER, Max
Concertino
Maurer (1959)

BREUER, Karl Günther (1926-)
Atonalyse I. Spiel mit 12 Tönen in Variationsform [vla, str orch]
Sikorski (1957)

BRIXI, František Xaver
Concerto in C. See Viola with Keyboard

BROTT, Alexander (1915-)
Profundum praedictum (1964) [vla, str orch or vlc, str orch, or str bs, str orch]
*Canadian (loan)

BRUCH, Max (1838-1920)
Canzone, Op. 55 [orig: vlc, orch]
Breitkopf

Romance in F, Op. 85 [orig: vln, orch]
Schott (1911)

BRUMBY, Colin James (1933-)
Concertino [vla, str orch]
*CompGuildGB (r)

BRUSTAD, Bjarne (1895-)
Concertino
NorskKomp

BÜSSER, Paul Henri (1872-1973)
Rhapsodie arménienne, Op. 81 [vla, orch or vla, pno]
*Leduc (r)

BUNIN, Revol Samuilovich
Concerto, Op. 22. *See* Viola with Keyboard

BURKHARD, Willy (1900-1955)
Concerto (1953)
*Bärenreiter (1954)

CAMPAGNOLI, Bartolomeo (1751-1827)
Berühmte Romanze [vla, str orch; orig: vln, str orch]
SchmidtCF

CASADESUS, François Louis (1870-1954)
Morceau de concert
*Salabert (r)

CASTRO, Washington (1909-)
Concerto elegíaco (1950)
Ms

CAZDEN, Norman (1914-)
Concerto, Op. 103
*MCA

CHAĬKOVSKIĬ, Petr Il'ich (1840-1893)
Chant sans paroles, Op. 2, No. 3 [vla, str orch; orig: pno]
SchmidtCF (Beda)

CIMAROSA, Domenico (1749-1801)
Concerto [vla, str orch]
Boosey

CLARKE, Henry Leland (1907-)
Encounter
*AmCompAll

COHN, Arthur (1910-)
Suite, Op. 28a
Elkan-Vogel

COLLET, Henri (1885-1951)
Rapsodie castillane, Op. 73
*Senart (1925) (r)

COOLEY, Carlton (1898-)
Concertino
ElkanH

COOPER, Walter Thomas Gaze (1895-   )

>*Concerto*, Op. 85 (1961)
>*CompGuildGB (r)

CORUM, Alfred (1890-1969)

>*Concerto*, Op. 21 (1965)
>*CompGuildGB (r)

CURTI, Franz

>*Klagelied*, Op. 41, No. 2 [vla, chamb orch]
>Seeling

DAVID, Gyula (1913-   )

>*Concerto*
>*Budapest (r)
>Zenemükiado (1953)

DAVID, Johann Nepomuk (1895-   )

>*Melancholia*, Op. 53 (1958) [vla, str orch]
>Breitkopf (1959)
>*Doblinger

DEGEN, Helmut (1911-   )

>*Kleines Konzert No. 3*
>Schott (1946)

DE JONG, Marinus (1891-   )

>*Concerto*, Op. 111
>Belgian

DELLO JOIO, Norman (1913-)
Lyric Fantasies [vla, str orch or vla, str quar]
*Associated (1975)

DE MEESTER, Louis (1904-)
Magreb
Ms

DEMUTH, Norman Frank (1898-1968)
Concerto
Ms

DISPA, Robert
Concerto (1970-1971) [vla, str orch]
*Donemus (1973)

DITTERS VON DITTERSDORF, Karl (1739-1799)
Concerto No. 1 in G
Breitkopf (1776-1777)
Concerto No. 2 in E-flat
Breitkopf (1776-1777)
Concerto No. 3 in F, Krebs No. 168
Breitkopf (1776-1777)
*Schott (Lebermann)

DODGSON, Stephen (1924-)
Serenade
Ms

DOMAZLICKÝ, Frantisek
Concerto, Op. 36
*Panton (r)

DONATO, Anthony (1909-)

Sonnet (1946) [vla, chamb orch or clar, chamb orch]
AmCompAll

DOPPELBAUER, Josef

Concerto. See Viola with Keyboard

DUBOIS, Théodore

Suite de danses. See Viola with Keyboard

DUNHILL, Thomas Frederick (1877-1946)

Tryptych, Op. 99
*Oxford (1949) (r)

DUPORT, Jean-Louis (1749-1819)

Romance [vla, str orch; orig: vlc, str orch]
SchmidtCF (Klemeke)

DYSON, Sir George (1833-1964)

Prelude, Fantasy and *Chaconne*
Novello (1936)

EISNER, C.

Pièces de salon (2), Op. 16
Hofmeister (1863)

ERDTEL, Frohwald

Variations on a Scandinavian Folksong (ca. 1930)
Ms

ERNST, Heinrich Wilhelm (1814-1865)

Elégie, Op. 10 [vla, str orch; orig: vln, str orch]
SchmidtCF (Pagels)

ERSFELD, C.

Ständchen, Op. 10 [vla, str orch; orig: vln, str orch]
Simon

FELDMAN, Morton (1926-)

The Viola in My Life IV
*Universal (r)

FERNSTRÖM, John Axel (1897-1961)

Concerto, Op. 34
Ms
Romance in c-sharp
Ms

FISCHER, Jan F. (1921-)

Concerto, Op. 10 (1946)
Ms

FORSYTH, Cecil (1870-1941)

Chanson celtique
Schott (1906)
Concerto in g
Schott (1910)

FORTNER, Wolfgang (1907-)

Concertino in g (1934) [vla, chamb orch]
Schott (1934)

FOSS, Lukas (1922-   )
  Orpheus (1972)
  *Salabert

FRANCAIX, Jean René Désiré (1912-   )
  Rhapsody (1946)
  Schott (1952)

FRANCK, Maurice (1897-   )
  Suite
  *Transatlantiques (r)
  Theme and Variations
  *Durand (1957) (r)

FRANKE, G.
  Fantasy [vla, str orch; orig: euphonium, str orch]
  Seeling

FRANKEL, Benjamin (1906-1973)
  Concerto, Op. 45 (1962)
  *Novello (r)

FREED, Isadore (1900-1960)
  Rhapsody
  *Fischer (r)

FRICKER, Peter Racine (1920-   )
  Concerto, Op. 20 (1952)
  Schott (1953)

FRID, Grigory S.

Concerto. See **Viola with Keyboard**

GARCIN, Jules (1830- ?)

Concertino, Op. 19
    Lemoine (1870)

GENZMER, Harald (1909-)

Chamber Concerto [vla, str orch]
    *Peters
Concerto
    *Eulenburg
Notturno [vla, str orch or hn, str orch]
    *Eulenburg

GERHARD, Fritz Christian (1911-)

Concerto (1954)
    *Möseler (Hoffmann)

GERSTER, Ottmar (1897-)

Concertino, Op. 16 [vla, chamb orch]
    Schott (1930)
Concerto. See **Viola with Keyboard**

GERVASIO, N.

Feuilles de printemps
    Decourcelle (1904)

GHEBART, Joseph (1796- ?)

Concerto No. 1, Op. 55
    Costallat (ca. 1830)

GHEDINI, Giorgio Federico (1892-1965)

Musica da concerto [vla, orch or vla d'amore, orch]
*Ricordi (r)

GIORNOVICCHI, Giovanni Mane (ca. 1735-1804)

Concerto No. 1 in D
Janet (Breval)

GIRANECK, [?]

Concerto in G
Breitkopf (1762)

GIUFFRÉ, Gaetano

Concerto
*Ricordi (r)

GIVOTOWSKI, T.

Konzertstück in d (ca. 1930)
Ms

GLANVILLE-HICKS, Peggy (1912-)

Concerto romantico
*Peters (r)

GLAZUNOV, Aleksandr Konstantinovich (1865-1936)

Concerto
RussSt (1948)
Elegy in g, Op. 44
*Belaieff (r)

GOCK, E.

Friede im Herzen, Op. 21 [vla, chamb orch]
Oertel

GOLESTAN, Stan (1875-1956)

Arioso and Allegro de concert
*Salabert (r)

GOLUBEV, Evgenii Kirillovich

Concerto, Op. 47. *See* Viola with Keyboard

GOOSEN, Frederic

Concerto
*AmCompAll (r)

GOULD, Morton (1913-)

Concertette (1940)
Mills
Concerto
*Belwin-Mills (r)

GRAF, C. E.

Concerto No. 1 in G
Breitkopf (1778)

GREENWOOD, John Darnforth Herman (1889-)

Concerto
Ms

GRENZER, [?]

Concerto No. 1 in G
Breitkopf (1882-1884)

GRETCHANINOV, Alexander Tikhonovitch (1864-1956)
Berceuse, Op. 1, No. 5 [vla, chamb orch]
Belaieff

GROSS, Paul (1898-)
Concerto
Ms

GUARNIERI, Mozart Camargo (1907-)
Choro
Ms

GUÉNIN, Marie Alexandre (1744-1835)
Concerto No. 1 in D, Op. 14
Sieber

HÁBA, Alois (1893-)
Concerto, Op. 86
Cesky

HÄRTEL, A.
Ständchen [vla, str orch]
Seeling

HANDEL, George Frideric (1685-1759)
Concerto [compilation] [vla, str orch]
*Oxford (Barbirolli)
Concerto in b [compilation]
*Eschig (Casadesus)
Concerto in g. See **Viola with Keyboard**
Largo, from *Xerxes* [vla, str orch; orig: voice, str orch]
SchmidtCF (Wellmann)
Simon (Wellmann)

HANNUSCH, Franz

> *Der Hoffnungslose: Fantasie* [vla, str orch]
> Hannusch (1896)

HANSON, Howard (1896-)

> *Summer Seascape No. 2* [vla, str orch]
> *Fischer (r)
> *Symphonic Poem "Lux aeterna,"* Op. 22 (1923) [vla obbligato]
> Schirmer

HARTMANN, Karl Amadeus

> *Concerto.* *See* Viola with Keyboard

HASENÖHRL, Franz (1885-)

> *Concerto*
> Ms

HAUG, Hans

> *Fantasia concertante.* *See* Viola with Keyboard

HAWTHORNE-BAKER, Allan (ca. 1910-)

> *Concerto in e*
> Hinrichsen

HAY, Frederick Charles (1888-1945)

> *Concerto in a*, Op. 16
> Tischer (1928)

HAYDN, Franz Joseph (1732-1809)

> *Concerto in D*, Hob. VIIb/2 [orig: vlc, orch]
> *Boosey (Tertis) (r)

HAYDN, Michael

Concerto in C. See **Viola with Keyboard**

HENKEMANS, Hans (1913-   )

Concerto (1954)
*Donemus (r)
*Eulenburg

HILL, Alfred Francis (1870-1960)

Concerto
*Peer-Southern (r)

HINDEMITH, Paul (1895-1963)

Concerto, Op. 48 (1930) [vla, chamb orch]
*Schott (1931) (r)
Kammermusik No. 5: Concerto, Op. 36, No. 4 (1927) [vla, chamb orch]
    Associated
*Schott (1928)
Der Schwanendreher (1935) [vla, chamb orch]
*Schott (1935)
Trauermusik (1936) [vla, str orch or vlc, str orch or vln, str orch]
*Schott (1936)

HODDINOTT, Alun (1929-   )

Concertino [vla, chamb orch]
*Oxford (r)

HOFFMEISTER, Franz Anton (1754-1812)

Concerto in D
*Grahl (r)
*International (r)

HOFSTETTER, Romanus (1742-1815)

Concerto in C
  *Schott (Lebermann)
Concerto in G
  Breitkopf (1785-1787)
Concerto No. 1 in E-flat
  Breitkopf (1785-1787)

HOLST, Gustav Theodore (1874-1934)

Lyric Movement [vla, chamb orch]
  *Oxford (r)

HOLZHAUS, H.

Elegy, Op. 2 [vla, str orch; orig: vln, str orch]
  SchmidtCF (Pagels)

HONEGGER, Arthur (1892-1955)

Concerto
  Ms

HONNORÉ, Leon

Morceau de concert
  *Gilles (Waël/Munk) (r)

HOVHANESS, Alan (1911-)

Concerto [vla, str orch]
  AmCompAll
Talin. Concerto, Op. 93 [vla, str orch]
  *Associated

HOWELLS, Herbert (1892-)

Elegy, Op. 15 (1917) [vla, str orch or vla, str quar]
  Boosey

HÜBSCHMANN, C.

Variations in E-flat
Breitkopf (1830)

HÜBSCHMANN, Werner (1901-   )

Concerto (1928)
Ms

HÜE, Georges-Adolphe (1858-1948)

Thème varié
Heugel (1922)

HUGGLER, John (1928-   )

Divertimento, Op. 32
*Peters (r)

HUMMEL, Johann Nepomuk (1778-1837)

Fantasy [vla, str orch]
*Transatlantiques

HUSA, Karel (1921-   )

Poem (1959) [vla, chamb orch]
Schott

IMELMANN, Heinrich (1866-   )

Wiegenlied, Op. 6 [vla, str orch]
Lehne

INDY, Vincent d' (1851-1931)

Lied, Op. 19 [orig: vlc, orch]
*International (r)

JACOB, Gordon Percival Septimus (1895-)

Concerto (1925)
*Oxford (1926) (r)

JACOBY, Hanoch

Concertino. See **Viola with Keyboard**

JAROCH, Jiři (1920-)

Fantasy
*Artia
*Panton (r)

JESINGHAUS, Walter (1902-)

Concerto, Op. 37 (1936)
Ms

JOLAS, Betsy (1926-)

Points d'aube [vla, 13 winds]
*Heugel (1969) (r)

JONGEN, Joseph (1873-1953)

Allegro appassionato, Op. 79 (1925)
*Leduc (r)
Suite en deux parties, Op. 48 (1915)
Lemoine

JOSEPHS, Wilfred (1927-)

Meditatio de beornmundo, Op. 30
*Weinberger (r)

JÜTTNER, Oskar

> *Légende* [vla, str orch]
> SchmidtCF (Pagels)
> *Mazurka*, Op. 26, No. 2 [vla, str orch]
> SchmidtCF
> *Serenade*, Op. 21 [vla, str orch]
> SchmidtCF

JULLIEN, René (1878-)

> *Concertstück in C*, Op. 19
> Simrock (1919)

KADOSA, Pál (1903-)

> *Concertino*, Op. 27
> *Boosey

KALAŠ, Julius (1902-)

> *Concerto in d*, Op. 69
> *Panton (r)

KALLSTENIUS, Edvin (1881-1967)

> *Cavatina*, Op. 30
> Ms

KEGEL, Karl (1770- ?)

> *Eine Sommernacht. Nocturne*, Op. 78 [vla, chamb orch]
> Bellmann

KELEMEN, Milko (1924-)

> *Dances* (3) [vla, str orch]
> *Universal (r)

KHANDOSHKIN, Ivan Evstaf'evich (1747-1804)
Concerto in C
   *International (r)
   Leeds
   *MezhdKniga (r)

KISTLER, Cyrill (1848-1907)
Serenade, Op. 72 [vla, chamb orch]
   Simon

KITTLER, Richard (1924-)
Concerto
   EdDAP

KLENNER, John
Fantasia. See Viola with Keyboard

KLOSE, Oskar (1859-)
Salve regina (*Andante religioso*), Op. 43 [vla, chamb orch]
   SchmidtCF

KÖLLE, Konrad
Concerto in A, Op. 38. *See* Viola with Keyboard

KOHS, Ellis Bonoff (1916-)
Chamber Concerto (1949) [vla, 9 strings]
   AmCompAll
   *Merrymount (r)

KOHSER, E.
Abendglöckchen. Romance, Op. 9 [vla, str orch; orig: vln, str orch]
   Seeling

KOPPRASCH, Wilhelm

Introduction and Variations
    Ms

KRANZ, Johann Friedrich (1752-1810)

Concerto No. 1 in B-flat
    Breitkopf (1779-1780)

KRAUSE, [?]

Concerto No. 1 [vla, str orch]
    Breitkopf (1767)

KREJČÍ, Miroslav (1891-1964)

Capriccio, Op. 83 (1950) [vla, wind insts]
    Ms
Concerto in E, Op. 72 (1947)
    Cesky

KREUZ, Emil (1867-)

Barcarole, from *Concerto*, Op. 20
    Augener (1896)
Concerto in C, Op. 20
    Augener (1893)

KRIEGER, Edino (1928-)

Brasiliana (1960) [vla, str orch]
    Ms

KÜFFNER, Joseph (1776-1856)

Concerto, Op. 139
    Schott (1823)
Potpourri in D, Op. 57
    André (1816)

KURTÁG, György (1926-)
Concerto
  *Budapest (r)

KURTZWEIL, Franz
  Concerto in B-flat
  Ms

KVAPIL, Jaroslav (1892-1958)
  Suite (1955)
  Ms

LANG, Walter (1896-1966)
  Variationen über ein sibirisches Sträflingslied, Op. 28
  Ms

LAPARRA, Raoul (1876-1943)
  Suite ancienne en marge de "Don Quichotte"
  Heugel (1921)

LARSSON, Lars Erik Vilner (1908-)
  Concertino No. 9, Op. 45 (1956) [vla, str orch]
  Gehrmans (r)

LATANN, C.
  Am Kamin. Romance, Op. 244 [vla, str orch; orig: vlc, str orch]
  Benjamin

LAVALLE GARCIA, Armando (1924-)
  Concerto (1965) [vla, str orch]
  Ms

LEDENER, Roman Semenovich
Concerto-Poem, Op. 13. *See* Viola with Keyboard

LEICHTLING, Alan (1947-   )
Concerto
*Seesaw

LEONCAVALLO, Ruggiero (1858-1919)
Serenade [vla, str orch]
Brockhaus (Hermann)

LEY, Salvador (1907-   )
Concertante (1962) [vla, str orch]
Ms

LINK, Emil
Chant d'amour. Mélodie romantique [vla, str orch]
SchmidtCF

LONGUE, Georges (1900-   )
Concerto No. 1
Ms
Concerto No. 2 in d, Op. 15 (*"Romantique"*)
Bode-Vinck
Images d'orient, Op. 20 (1935)
Leduc

LO PRESTI, Ronald (1933-   )
Nocturne [vla, str orch]
*Fischer

LORENZITI, Bernardo (1764- ?)

Concerto
  Boyer (ca. 1764)

LUTYENS, Elisabeth

Concerto. See **Viola with Keyboard**

McCABE, John (1939-)

Concerto funebre (1962) [vla, chamb orch]
  *Novello (r)

MACONCHY, Elisabeth (1907-)

Concerto
  *Lengnick (r)
  Oxford

MAES, Jef

Concerto. See **Viola with Keyboard**

MALIGE, Fred (1895-)

Concerto
  Breitkopf (1955)

MALIPIERO, Gian Francesco (1882-1973)

Dialoghi-V
  *Ricordi (r)

MANNS, Ferdinand (1844- ?)

Romance in G, Op. 31
  Benjamin (1899)

MARTINU, Bohuslav (1890-1959)

 Rhapsody-Concerto (1954)
  Boosey

MARX, Karl (1897-   )

 Concerto, Op. 10
  *Bote&Bock (1931) (r)
  Schott

MASSIS, Amable (1893-   )

 Poème
  *Billaudot (r)

MAUGÜE, J. M. L.

 Allegro, *Lento*, *Scherzo*
  Lemoine (1927)

MAURER, Louis Wilhelm (1789-1878)

 Divertimento, Op. 85 [vla, str orch]
  Peters

MAZAS, Jacques Féréol (1782-1849)

 La Consolation. Elégie in G, Op. 29
  Pleyel (1831)
 Elegy in C, Op. 73
  Benjamin (1899)

MEESTER, Louis de (1904-   )

 Magreb (1946)
  Belgian

MEJO, W.

Concertino in C [vla, str orch]
Häcker

MENDELSSOHN, Arnold Ludwig (1855-1933)

Student Concerto in D, Op. 213 (1st movement) [orig: vlc, orch]
*Fischer (Klotman)

MERIGHI, Vincenzo (1795- ?)

Concertino in D
Ricordi (ca. 1840)

MEULEMANS, Arthur (1884-1966)

Concerto (1942)
Belgian

MEYER, Clemens (1868-)

Romance, Op. 6
Benjamin (1899)

MEYER, Ernst Herman

Poem. See Viola with Keyboard

MEYER, Karl Walter (1902-)

Kleines Konzert [vla, chamb orch]
Ms

MEYER-OLBERSLEBEN, Max

Concerto, Op. 112. *See* Viola with Keyboard

MICHL, Giuseppe

Concerto No. 1 in G
    Breitkopf (1782-1784)

MIHELIČ, Pavle (1937-)

Moderato cantabile [vla, chamb orch]
    *Društva

MIKHASHOFF, Yvar-Emilian

Concerto
    Ms

MILETIĆ, Miroslav (1925-)

Concerto
    Ms

MILFORD, Robin Humphrey (1903-1959)

Elegiac Meditation [vla, str orch]
    Oxford

MILHAUD, Darius (1892-1974)

Concerto (1929)
    *Universal (r)
Concerto No. 2
    *Heugel (r)

MIMAROGLU, Ilhan Kemaleddin (1926-)

Idols of Perversity [vla, str orch]
    *Seesaw

MOÓR, Emanuel (1863-1931)
Konzertstück in c-sharp
Ms

MOREY, George
Celtic Suite
Ms

MORGAN, David Sydney (1932-)
Concerto, Op. 19 (1958) [vla, str orch]
Ms

MORTARI, Virgilio (1902-)
Concerto dell'osservanza
*Ricordi (r)

MOSER, Rudolf (1892-1960)
Concerto, Op. 62 (1934-1935)
Ms

MOZART, Johann Chrysostom Wolfgang Amadeus (1756-1791)
Larghetto [vla, str orch]
SchmidtCF (Pagels)

MÜLLER-ZÜRICH, Paul (1898-)
Concerto in F, Op. 24 [vla, chamb orch]
Schott (1935)

MUSGRAVE, Thea (1928-)
Concerto (1973)
Ms

NERUDA, Franz Xaver (1843-1915)

Berceuse slave d'apres un chant polonais, Op. 11 [vla, chamb orch; orig: vln, chamb orch]
Benjamin

NIVERD, Lucien

Concerto romantique. See **Viola with Keyboard**

NOBRE, Marlos (1939-)

Desafio, Op. 31 (1968) [vla, str orch]
SDMBrazil
*Tonos

NORDGREN, H. Erik (1913-)

Arioso, Op. 2
Ms

NOSSEK, Karl

Près du Léman, Abend am Genfer See. Rêverie, Op. 28 [vla, str orch]
Oertel
Im einsamen Fischerkahn. Seul! En bateau. Barkarole, Op. 27 [vla, str orch; orig: vln, pno]
Oertel (Gock)

NUSSIO, Otmar (1902-)

Notturno di Valdemosa
*Universal (r)

NYSTRÖM, Gösta (1890-1966)

Homage alla France. Concerto
Breitkopf
Svenska

OVERHOFF, Kurt (1902-)

Concerto
Ms

PARRIS, Robert (1924-)

Concerto (1956)
*AmCompAll

PARTOS, Oedoen (1907-)

Fusions-Shiluvim
*IsMusInst (r)
Sinfonia concertante. Concerto No. 3
*IsMusInst (r)
Yiskor. See **Viola with Keyboard**

PERLE, George (1915-)

Serenade No. 1 (1962) [vla, chamb orch]
*Presser (r)

PESCH, [?]

Concerto No. 1
Breitkopf (1774)

PINELLI, Carlo (1911-)

Concerto
*Ricordi (r)

PINZON-URREA, Jesus (1928-)

Concerto (1971)
Ms

PISK, Paul Amadeus (1893-   )

Baroque Chamber Concerto (Eccles/Valentini) [vla, chamb orch]
*Peer-Southern (Pisk) (r)

PISTON, Walter Hamor (1894-1976)

Concerto (1957)
*Associated (r)

PLEYEL, Ignaz Joseph (1757-1831)

Concerto in D, Op. 31
*Grahl (Hermann)

POLAND, Theo

Concertino
Ms

PORTER, Quincy (1897-1966)

Concerto (1948)
*Associated (r)

PRÄGER, Heinrich Aloys (1783-   ?)

Concerto
Ms

PREUS, [?]

Concerto No. 1 in B-flat
Breitkopf (1785-1787)
Concerto No. 2 in B-flat
Breitkopf (1785-1787)

PREZUHN, Alex (1870-   )
Concerto
  Ms

PROSZNITZ, Anatol
Fantasy (1934)
  Ms

PURSER, John Whitley (1942)
Concerto, Op. 14 (1966) [vla, str orch]
  *CompGuildGB (r)

QUINET, Marcel
Concerto. *See* Viola with Keyboard

RANK, W.
Ave Maria, Op. 15 [vla, str orch]
  Haslinger

RAWSTHORNE, Alan (1905-1971)
Concerto
  Hinrichsen (1956)

READ, Gardner (1913-   )
Fantasy, Op. 38 (1935)
  *Associated (r)
Poem, Op. 31
  *Fischer (r)

REBNER, Edward Wolfgang (1910-   )
Virtuose legende
  *Moderne (r)

REED, Alfred (1921-   )

Rhapsody
    *Boosey (r)

REICHA, Joseph (1746-1795)

Concerto in E-flat, Op. 2
    Simrock

RENOSTO, Paolo (1935-   )

Scops. Strutture e improvvisazioni
    *Ricordi (r)

RETTICH, Wilhelm (1892-   )

Suite in Old Style, Op. 40 [vla, str orch]
    Novello (1952)

RICHTER, Marga (1926-   )

Air and Toccata [vla, str orch]
    Mills

RIDOUT, Godfrey (1918-   )

Ballade (1938)
    *Canadian (loan)

RIETH, Wilhelm (1906-   )

Pieces (2) [vla, chamb orch]
    Ms

RITTER, Hermann (1849-1926)

Concert Fantasy No. 2 in C, Op. 36
    Kistner (1886)
Schlummerlied, Op. 9 [vla, str orch; orig: vln, str orch]
    Simrock

RIVIER, Jean (1896-)

Concertino
  *Senart (r)

RODERICK-JONES, Richard (1947-)

Concerto (1967)
  *CompGuildGB (r)

ROE, Christopher John (1940-)

Concerto (1960)
  *CompGuildGB (r)

ROGISTER, Jean (1879-1964)

Concerto No. 1
  Ms

ROLLA, Alessandro (1757-1841)

Adagio e Tema con Variazioni
  Günther
  Ricordi
  *Suvini-Zerboni (Bianchi) (1977)
Concertino in E-flat [vla, orch or vla, str quar]
  Lucca
Concerto in D
  Ms (Milan)
Concerto in F
  *Santis (Centurioni) (1970)
Concerto in F
  Günther (Schaller) (1936)
Concerto in E-flat, Op. 3 (1st version)
  Ms (Milan)
Concerto in E-flat, Op. 3 (2nd version)
  André (1800)
  *Ricordi (Beck) (1953)

Concerto in F, Op. 4
    André (1799)
Concerto No. 3 in E-flat
    Ms (Milan)
Concerto No. 4 in C
    Ms (Milan)
Concerto in B-flat
    Ms (Milan)
Concerto in D (*Konzertstück*) [orchestration incomplete]
    Ms (Milan)
Concerto No. 5a in E (*Konzertstück*)
    Ms (Milan)
Divertimento in F [vla, str orch]
    Ms (Milan)
Rondo in G
    *Rarities for Strings (Sciannameo) (1977)

ROLLA, Antonio (1798-1837)

Variations brillantes, Op. 13 [vla, str orch]
    Ricordi

ROOS, Robert de (1907-   )

Concerto (1940-1941)
    Donemus (1949)

ROPARTZ, Joseph Guy Marie (1864-1955)

Adagio
    Rouart (ca. 1925)

ROSENBERG, Hilding Constantin (1892-   )

Concerto (1942) [vla, str orch]
    Nordiska
Ett litet Stycke
    Suecia

ROSINSKÝ, Jozef

Sonatina [vla, str orch]
*Slovenský

ROUGNON, Paul

Concerto romantique, Op. 138. *See* **Viola with Keyboard**

ROUSSEL, Albert Charles Paul (1869-1937)

Aria
Leduc

RUBBRA, Edmund (1901-)

Concerto in A, Op. 75
*Lengnick (r)

RÜDIGER, S.

Concerto No. 1 in C, Op. 1
Simrock (1870)

RUTHENFRANZ, R.

Partita
Maurer

RUYGROK, Leo (Leonard Petrus) (1889-1944)

Poeme. Fantasiestück, Op. 20
Ms

SALGADO, Luis Humberto (1903-)

Concerto in F (1955-1956)
Ms

SANTÓRSOLA, Guido (1904-)

Canción triste y danza brasileña (1934)
Ms
Concerto (1933)
*Peer-Southern (r)
Sonata, de Ariosti (1934) [vla, chamb orch]
Ms
Sonata-Fantasia (1938) [vla, orch or vln, orch or vlc, orch]
Ms

SAPIEYEVSKI, Jerzy (1945-)

Concerto (1971) [vla, winds]
*Presser (r)

SCHÄFER, Karl (1899-)

Divertimento on a Theme by Conrad Paumann [vla, chamb orch or vln,
chamb orch]
*Gerig

SCHAEUBLE, Hans-Joachim (1906-)

Music, Op. 23 (1938-1939)
Bote&Bock (1940)

SCHERCHEN, Tona (1938-)

Tao
*Universal (r)

SCHIBLER, Armin (1920-)

Fantasy, Op. 15 (1946)
Ahn&Sim (1956)

SCHMIDT, Walter (1883-)

Concerto (ca. 1930)
Ms

SCHMITT, Florent (1870-1958)

Legende, Op. 66 [vla, orch or sax, orch]
*Durand (r)

SCHÖNBURG, G.

Auf der Wolga, Op. 43 [vla, str orch]
SchmidtCF
Mein Abschied aus Georgien, Op. 34 [vla, str orch]
SchmidtCF (Pagels)

SCHROEDER, Hermann (1904-)

Concerto (1974)
*Gerig

SCHUBERT, Joseph (1757- ?)

Concerto in C
*Schott (Schultz/Hauser)

SCHULTZE, Louis

Danse russe. Burleske [vla, chamb orch; orig: vln, chamb orch]
Oertel

SCHUMAN, William Howard (1910-)

Concerto on Old English Rounds (1974) [vla, women's chor, orch]
*Merion

SCHUMANN, Robert Alexander (1810-1856)
  Abendlied, Op. 85, No. 12 [vla, str orch; orig: pno 4 hands]
    SchmidtCF (Meyer)

SEEMANN, Helmut (1921-   )
  Concerto [vla, chamb orch]
    Schott (Banks) (1954)

SEIBER, Mátyás György (1905-1960)
  Elegy
    *Schott

SERLY, Tibor (1900-   )
  Concerto. See Viola with Keyboard
  Rhapsody on Folksongs Harmonized by Béla Bartók
    *Peer-Southern (r)

SETER, Mordecai (1916-   )
  Elegy
    *IsMusInst (r)

SHULMAN, Alan (1915-   )
  Theme and Variations (1940)
    Chappell

SIMONS, Netty (1913-   )
  Illuminations in Space (1972)
    Merion

SITT, Hans (1850-1922)
  Concerto in a, Op. 68. *See* Viola with Keyboard
  Konzertstück in g, Op. 46
    *International (r)

ŠKERJANC, Lucijan Marija (1900-)

Koncertna rapsodija
*Društva

SKÖLD, Yngve (1899-)

Suite, Op. 53
Svenska

SMIT, Leo (1921-)

Concerto (1940)
Donemus

SOBANSKI, Hans Joachim (1906-)

Romantic Concerto
*Universal (r)

SOMERVILLE, Horace

Concerto in One Movement
Ms

SOPRONI, József

Concerto. *See* Viola with Keyboard

SORIANO, Alberto (1915-)

Homenaje a Dresden (ca. 1967)
Ms

SOWERBY, Leo (1895-1968)

Concerto
Gray

SPANNAGEL, Carl

Concerto. See Viola with Keyboard

SPIREA, Andrei

Symphonie de chambre. See Viola with Keyboard

STAMITZ, Anton (1754-1809)

Concerto in B-flat. See Viola with Keyboard
Concerto No. 2 in F
  Breitkopf (1774)
Concerto No. 3 in G
  *Breitkopf (r)
Concerto No. 4 in D [vla, str orch]
  *Bärenreiter

STAMITZ, Johann Wenzel Anton (1717-1757)

Concerto in G
  *Eulenburg
  *Peters (Laugg)

STAMITZ, Karl (1745-1801)

Concerto No. 1 in D, Op. 1
  *Eulenburg
  International
  *Peters (Soldan) (r)
Concerto No. 2 in D. See Viola with Keyboard

STARER, Robert (1924-)

Concerto (1958) [vla, str orch, perc]
  *MCA (r)

STEINER, George (1900-1967)

Rhapsodic Poem
  Leeds
  *MCA (r)

STEINER, Hugo von (1862-)

Concerto in d, Op. 43. *See* **Viola with Keyboard**
Concerto, Op. 44. *See* **Viola with Keyboard**
Concerto No. 3 in a, Op. 51. *See* **Viola with Keyboard**

STEWART, Robert J. (1918-)

Fantasia
  *AmCompAll

STRATTON, George (1897-1954)

Concerto pastorale (1959)
  Boosey

SUCHY, František (1891-)

Vintner's Suite
  *Artia (r)

SVEINSSON, Atli Heimir (1938-)

Concerto
  *Islenzk (r)

SVENSSON, Sven Erik Emanuel (1899-1960)

Concerto in One Movement
  Ms

SYDEMAN, William (1928-)

Concerto da camera
  *Seesaw

Music
  *Okra

SZEREMI, Gustav

Concerto No. 1 in F, Op. 6
  Rosznyai (1908)
Concerto No. 2 in B-flat, Op. 57
  Rosznyai (1911)

TAL, Joseph

Concerto. See **Viola with Keyboard**

TANSMAN, Alexander (1897-   )

Concerto (1936)
  Ms

TARTINI, Giuseppe (1692-1770)

Concerto in D [orig: vln, orch]
  Eschig
  Schott (Vieux/Dumont)

TAUTENHAHN, Gunther

Concerto [vla, chamb orch]
  *Seesaw

TELEMANN, Georg Philipp (1681-1767)

Concerto in G [vla, str orch]
  *Bärenreiter (Wolff)
  Breitkopf (1762)
  *International (r)
Suite in D [vla, str orch or vl da gamba, str orch or vlc, str orch]
  *Möseler (Hoffmann)

TESTI, Flavio (1923-)

Musica da concerto No. 6, Op. 20 [vla, chamb orch]
*Ricordi

THADEWALDT, Hermann (1827-1909)

Abendständchen, Op. 20 [vla, str orch; orig: vln, str orch]
SchmidtCF

TICCIATI, Niso (1924-1972)

Suite [vla, chamb orch]
Ms

TLIL, Amali

Concerto
*Jobert (r)

TOMASI, Henri-Frédien (1901-1971)

Concerto
Leduc (1950)

TÓMASSON, Jonas (1881-)

Concerto
*Islenzk (r)

URIBE-HOLGUÍN, Guillermo (1880-)

Concerto, Op. 109
Ms

VACTOR, David van (1906-)

Concerto (1940)
Ms

VAN DER VELDEN, Renier (1910-   )

Chamber Music [vla, chamb orch]
*Belgian (r)

VAŇHAL, Jan Křtitel [Johann Baptist] (1732-1813)

Concertino in F
*Doblinger (Weinmann)
Concerto in C
*Panton (r)

VARDI, Emanuel (1915-   )

Suite on American Folk-Songs
*Schirmer (r)

VAUGHAN WILLIAMS, Ralph (1872-1958)

Flos campi [vla, chor, orch]
*Eulenburg
Oxford
Suite
*Oxford (r)

VERESS, Sándor (1907-   )

Ungarischer Werbetanz
*Universal (r)

VERRALL, John W. (1908-   )

Concerto
*AmCompAll

VISCONTI, Julio

Concerto in C
Ms

VIVALDI, Antonio (1678-1741)

Concerto in A
*Transatlantiques (r)
Concerto in b [vla, str orch]
*Fischer (Courte)
Concerto in d. See **Viola with Keyboard**
Concerto in e
*International (Primrose) (r)
Concerto in E [vla, str orch]
*Fischer (Courte)
Sonata No. 3 in a
*International (Primrose) (r)
Sonata No. 6 in B-flat
*International (Primrose) (r)

VOIGT, Johann Georg Hermann (1769- ?)

Concerto in C, Op. 11
André

VORLOVA, Slava

Slowakisches Konzert, Op. 35 (1954)
Ms

VYCPÁLEK, Ladislav (1882-)

Suite, Op. 21
*Artia

WALLNER, Leopold

Fantaisie de concert in d
Schott (1879)

WALTON, Sir William Turner (1902-)

Concerto (rev. 1962)
*Eulenburg
*Oxford (r)

WANHAL, Johann Baptist. *See* Vaňhal, Jan Křtitel

WEBER, Ben (1916-   )

   Rapsodie concertante, Op. 47 (1957) [vla, chamb orch]
      *AmCompAll

WESTERMANN, Helmut (1895-   )

   Konzertante Musik, Op. 34 [vla, str orch]
      Simrock (1958)

WHETTAM, Graham

   Concerto, Op. 16
      deWolfe (r)

WIGGLESWORTH, Frank (1918-   )

   Concertino
      *AmCompAll

WITNI, Monica (1928-   )

   Concerto in c
      Ms

WITTGENSTEIN, G. von

   A Peine au sortir, Romance from "Joseph" by Mehul
      André

WOLDEMAR, Michael (1750-   ?)

   Concerto
      Cochet (ca. 1816)

WOLF, Hugo (1860-1903)

Italian Serenade [vla, chamb orch; orig: str quar]
Associated
*Breitkopf

WOLFF, [?]

Concerto No. 1 in B-flat
Breitkopf

WOOLDRIDGE, David

Concerto
*MCA (r)

WRANITZKY, Anton (1761- ?)

Concerto
Ms

WYMAN, Dann

Ode to the Viola
*Seesaw

WYNNE, David (1900-)

Fantasia Concerto
Ms

YOUFEROFF, Sergei (1865-)

Melancolie, Op. 43
Schott (1910)

ZAFRED, Mario (1922-)

Concerto
*Ricordi (r)

Elegia
  *Ricordi (r)

ZEIDMAN, Boris Isaacovich

  Concerto No. 2. See **Viola with Keyboard**

ZELTER, Carl Friedrich (1758-1832)

  Concerto in E-flat
    *Eulenburg (1970)
    *Grahl (r)

ZIMMERMANN, Bernd Alois (1918-1970)

  Antiphonen
    *Moderne

ZONN, Paul

  Concerto for viola and 11 instruments
    Ms

ZUR LINDE, Karl

  Concerto (1929)
    Ms

LIST OF PUBLISHERS

Abbreviation	*Publisher*	*Agent/Distributor*
Affiliated	Affiliated Musicians, Inc. (Los Angeles)	
Ahn&Sim	Ahn & Simrock Meinekestrasse 10 Berlin, Germany *or* Schützenhofstrasse 4 Wiesbaden, West Germany	
Alsbach	Alsbach & Co. (Amsterdam)	Peters
Amadeus	Amadeus Verlag (Adliswil-Zürich)	Peters
AmCompAll	American Composers Alliance 170 West 74th Street New York, NY 10023	
AmMusCen	American Music Center 250 West 57th Street Suite 626-7 New York, NY 10019	
AmMusEd	American Music Edition	Fischer
André	Johann André Frankfurterstrasse 28 Offenbach am Main, West Germany	

333

Andrews	Andrews Music House 118 Main Street Bangor, ME 04401	
Anglo-French	Anglo-French Music Co. (London)	
Anglo-Soviet	Anglo-Soviet Music Press, Ltd. (London)	
ArsViva	Ars Viva Verlag (Vienna-Zürich-Milan)	Belwin-Mills
Artia	Artia Verlag (Prague)	Boosey
Artransa	Artransa Music	Western
Associated	Associated Music Publishers, Inc. 866 Third Avenue New York, NY 10022	
Astoria	Astoria-Verlag Brandenburgische Strasse 22 Berlin-Wilmersdorf, Germany	
Augener	Augener Editions (London)	Galaxy
Avant	Avant Music	Western
Azerb	Azerb. Gos. Muz. Izd. (Baku)	
Bärenreiter	Bärenreiter-Verlag (Kassel)	EuroAmer Magnamusic
Baltischer	Baltischer Musikverlag (Stettin)	
Belaieff	M. P. Belaieff (Bonn)	Peters
Belgian	Belgian Centre for Music Documentation (Brussels)	ElkanH
Bellmann	Bellmann und Thümer (Waldheim-Sachsen)	

Belwin-Mills	Belwin-Mills Publishing Corp. Melville, NY 11746	
Benjamin	Anton J. Benjamin (Hamburg) (later: SimBenjRaht)	
Bessel	Bessel & Cie. (Paris)	Belwin-Mills
Billaudot	Editions Billaudot (Paris)	Presser
Bisping	Ernst Bisping Ulmenallee 4132 Cologne-Bayenthal, West Germany	
Blake	Whitney Blake Music (New York)	
BMICan	BMI Canada Ltd.	Associated
Bode-Vinck	John Bode-Vinck Uitgever Anvers-12 Sint-Jacobsmarkt Antwerp, Belgium	
Bojer	Bojer (Paris)	
Bomart	Bomart Music Publications	Associated
Bongiovanni	F. Bongiovanni (Bologna)	Belwin-Mills
Boosey	Boosey & Hawkes, Inc. 30 West 57th Street New York, NY 10019	
Boston	Boston Music Company	Frank
Bosworth	Bosworth and Co., Ltd. 14/18 Heddon Street Regent Street London W1, England	
Bote&Bock	Bote & Bock (Wiesbaden-Berlin)	Associated

Bourne	Bourne Co. 1212 Ave. of the Americas New York, NY 10036	
Boyer	Pascal Boyer (Paris)	
Branch	Harold Branch Publishing, Inc. 42 Cornell Drive Plainview L.I., NY 11803	
Brandenburg	Theodor Brandenburg (Berlin)	Heinrichshofen
Breitkopf	Breitkopf & Härtel (Wiesbaden-Leipzig)	BroudeA
Brockhaus	Max Brockhaus (Leipzig)	
Brodt	Brodt Music Co. P. O. Box 1207 Charlotte, NC 28201	
Broekmans	Broekmans & Van Poppel (Amsterdam)	Peters
Brogneaux	Editions Musicales Brogneaux (Brussels)	ElkanH
Brook	Brook Publishing Co. 3602 Cedarbrook Road Cleveland Heights, OH 44118	
BroudeA	Alexander Broude, Inc. 225 West 57th Street New York, NY 10019	
BroudeBr	Broude Brothers Ltd. 56 West 45th Street New York, NY 10036	
Budapest	Editio Musica Budapest (Budapest)	Boosey

Buffet	Buffet-Crampon (Paris)	
Bulgarischer	Bulgarischer Staatsverlag (Sofia)	
Canadian	Canadian Music Centre 33 Edward Street Toronto 101, Ontario Canada	
Carisch	Carisch (Milan)	Boosey
Cesky	Cesky Hudebni Fond (Prague)	
Challier	C. A. Challier & Co. (Berlin)	
Chappell	Chappell & Co., Ltd. (London)	Presser
ChappellMus	Chappell Music Co. 609 Fifth Avenue New York, NY 10017	
Chester	J. and W. Chester Ltd. (London)	Magnamusic
Choudens	P. Choudens (Paris)	Peters
Church	John Church Co. (Philadelphia)	Presser
Cochet	Cochet (Paris)	
Colombo	Franco Colombo Inc.	Belwin-Mills
CompFacEd	Composers Facsimile Edition	AmCompAll
CompGuildGB	Composers Guild of Great Britain British Music Information Centre 10 Stratford Place London W1N 9AE England	
CompPr	Composers Press, Inc. Robert B. Brown Music Co. 1815 N. Kenmore Avenue Hollywood, CA 90028	

Comptoire	Comptoire de music moderne (Brussels)	
Concert	Concert Music Publishing Co.	Bourne
Concordia	Concordia Publishing House 3558 S. Jefferson Avenue St. Louis, MO 63118	
Consolidated	Consolidated Music Publishers Music Sales Corp. 33 West 60th Street New York, NY 10023	
Continuo	Continuo Music Press, Inc.	BroudeA
Cor	Cor Publishing Co. 67 Bell Place Massapequa L.I., NY	
Costallat	Costallat & Cie. (Paris)	Presser
Cramer	J. B. Cramer & Co., Ltd. (London)	BroudeA
Cranz	Editions Cranz (Wiesbaden)	ElkanH
Curci	Edizioni Curci Galleria del corso 4 Milan, Italy	
Curwen	J. Curwen & Sons (London)	Schirmer
David	David (Paris)	
Decourcelle	Paul Decourcelle (Nice)	
Deiro	Pietro Deiro Publications 133 Seventh Avenue New York, NY 10014	
Deiss	Deiss (Paris)	Salabert
Delrieu	George Delrieu & Cie. (Nice)	Galaxy

DeutschVerMus	Deutscher Verlag für Musik (Leipzig)	BroudeA
deWolfe	de Wolf (London)	
Diabelli	Diabelli (Vienna) (later: Cranz)	
Ditson	Oliver Ditson Co.	Presser
Doblinger	Ludwig Doblinger Verlag (Vienna)	Associated
Donemus	Stitchting Donemus (Amsterdam)	Peters
Draeseke	Draeseke Gesellschaft	
Drago	Edizioni Drago (Milan)	
Dresdner	Dresdner Verlag (Dresden)	
Društva	Edicije Društva slovenskih skladateljev Trg francoske revolucije 6 Ljubljana, Yugoslavia	Gerig
DruštvoHS	Društvo Hrvatskih Skladatelja Berislavičeva 9 Zagreb, Yugoslavia	
Durand	Durand & Cie. (Paris)	Presser
DuWast	Ulisse DuWast (Paris)	Salabert
EdCoopIntAm	Editorial Cooperativa Inter-Americana de Compositores (Montevideo)	Peer-Southern
EdDAP	Edition DAP Dr. Alfred Peschek Altdorferstrasse 3a 4050 St. Martin-Linz Austria	

Editura(Bucharest)	Editura de Stat pentru Literatura si Arta (Bucharest)	
ElkanH	Henri Elkan Music Publisher 1316 Walnut Street Philadelphia, PA 19107	
Elkan-Vogel	Elkan-Vogel, Inc.	Presser
Enoch	Enoch & Cie. (Paris)	Associated Peer-Southern
Eriks	Eriks Musikandel Och Förlag AB Karlavägen 40 Stockholm O, Sweden	
Eschig	Editions Max Eschig (Paris)	Associated
Etling	Forest R. Etling 1790 Joseph Court Elgin, IL 60120	
Eulenburg	Edition Eulenburg (London-Zürich-Mainz-New York)	Peters
EuroAmer	European American Music 195 Allwood Drive Clifton, NJ 07012	
ExpMusCat	Experimental Music Catalogue 208 Ladbroke Grove London W 10, England	
Fazer	Musik Fazer Postbox 260 00101 Helsinki 10, Finland	Magnamusic
Fema	Fema Music Publications P. O. Box 395 Naperville, IL 60540	

Fischer	Carl Fischer, Inc. 62 Cooper Square New York, NY 10003	
Foetisch	Foetisch Frères SA (Lausanne)	SchirmerEC
Forberg	Robert Forberg (Bad Godesburg)	Peters
Forlivesi	Forlivesi Via Roma 4 Florence, Italy	
Foster	Mark Foster Music Co. P. O. Box 4012 Champaign, IL 61820	
Fox	Sam Fox Publishing Co., Inc. P. O. Box 850 Valley Forge, PA 19482	
Francis	Francis, Day & Hunter, Ltd. 16 Soho Square London W 1, England	
Frank	Frank Music Corp. 116 Boylston Street Boston, MA 02116	
Frey	Frey (Paris)	
Fromont	Eugene Fromont (Paris) (later: Jobert)	
Fürstner	Adolf Fürstner (Berlin)	
Galaxy	Galaxy Music Corp. 2121 Broadway New York, NY 10023	
Gallet	Emile Gallet & Fils (Paris)	
Galliard	Galliard Ltd. (London)	Galaxy

Gamble	Gamble	
Gebauer	Wilhelm Gebauer (Leipzig)	
Gehrmans	Carl Gehrmans Musikförlag Vasagaten 46, Stockholm 1, Sweden	Boosey
General	General Music Publishing Co., Inc. (Hastings-on-Hudson, NY)	Schirmer
Gerig	Hans Gerig/Arno Volk Verlag (Cologne)	Belwin-Mills
Gilles	Gilles (Paris)	Salabert
Gleis	Gleis (Breslau)	
GosMusIzd	Gos. Mus. Izd. (Moscow-Leningrad)	
Grahl	Grahl (Frankfurt)	Peters
Gray	H. W. Gray Co., Inc. (New York)	Belwin-Mills
Greiner	Greiner (Moscow)	
Günther	Paul Günther Nostitzstrasse 41 Leipzig, East Germany	
Häcker	Häcker (Chemnitz)	
Hänssler	Hänssler (Stuttgart)	Peters
Hainauer	Julius Hainauer (Breslau)	
Hamelle	Hamelle & Cie. (Paris)	Presser
Hannusch	Hannusch (Forst i. L.)	
Hansen	Wilhelm Hansen, Musik-Forlag (Copenhagen-Frankfurt am Main)	Magnamusic

Harms	T. B. Harms (Santa Monica, CA)	Belwin-Mills
Hart	Hart (London)	
Haslinger	Carl Haslinger Tuchlauben 11 Vienna 1, Austria	
Hawkes	Hawkes & Sons (London) (later: Boosey & Hawkes)	
Heacox	Heacox	
Heinrichshofen	Heinrichshofen (Wilhelmshaven)	Peters
Helios	Editio Helios	Foster
Henmar	Henmar Press	Peters
Heugel	Heugel et Cie. (Paris)	Presser
Heuwekemeijer	Heuwekemeijer (Amsterdam)	Presser
Hieber	Musikverlag Max Hieber Kaufingerstrasse 23 8000 Munich 33, West Germany	
Highgate	Highgate Press	Galaxy
Hill	Hill (London)	
Hille	Hille, Weisser Hirsch (Dresden)	
Hinnenthal	Johann Philipp Hinnenthal Verlag (Kassel)	Bärenreiter
Hinrichsen	Hinrichsen Edition (London)	Peters
Hiob	Heinrich Hiob (Braunschweig) Paul Zschocher Isestrasse 117 Hamburg 13, West Germany	

Hofmeister	Friedrich Hofmeister (Hofheim am Taunus-Leipzig)	BroudeA
Holly-Pix	Holly-Pix Music Publishing Co.	Western
Hudebni	Hudebni matice umelecke Besedy (Prague)	
Hug	Hug & Co. (Zürich)	Peters
Hulpiau	Hulpiau 122 rue de la Clinique Brussels, Belgium	
Hymnophon	Hymnophon Alerts Musikverlag Lietzenburgerstrasse 15 Berlin W 15, Germany	
Impero	Impero Verlag (Wilhelmshaven)	Presser
InstExtMus	Instituto de Extensión Musical (Santiago)	
InstIntMus	Instituto Interamericano de Musicologia (Montevideo)	
International	International Music Company 511 Fifth Avenue New York, NY 10017	
Islensk	Islensk Tonverkamidstod (Iceland Music Information Center)	ElkanH
IsMusInst	Israeli Music Institute (Tel Aviv)	Boosey
IsMusPub	Israeli Music Publications, Ltd. (Tel Aviv)	BroudeA
Janet	Janet & Cotelle (Paris)	
Jobert	Editions Jean Jobert (Paris)	Presser

Jüdische	Verlag für Jüdische Musik (Moscow)	
Junne	Otto Junne GmbH Mittererstrasse 1 Munich 15, West Germany	
Jurgenson	P. Jurgenson (Moscow) (later: Forberg)	
Kahnt	C. F. Kahnt Musikverlag (Lindau)	Peters
Kallmeyer	Georg Kallmeyer K. G. Gr. Zimmerhof 20 Wolfenbüttel, West Germany	
Kalmus	Edwin F. Kalmus Orchestra Scores, Inc. P. O. Box 1007 13125 NW 47th Avenue Opa Locka, FL 33054	
Kistner	Kistner & Siegel Organum (Lippstadt)	Concordia
Kjos	Neil A. Kjos Music Co. 525 Busse Hwy. Park Ridge, IL 60068 *or* 4382 Jutland Drive San Diego, CA 92117	
Klett	Ernst Klett (Stuttgart)	
Krenn	Musikverlag Ludwig Krenn Reindorfgasse 42 1150 Vienna 15, Austria	
Kreyer	O. Kreyer (Krefeld)	
Kultura	Kultura (Ungarisches Aussenhandelsunternehmen) (Budapest)	Boosey
Langewiesche	Langewiesche (Iserlohn)	

Laudy	Laudy (London)	
Leduc	Alphonse Leduc (Paris)	Brodt SouthernTX
Leeds	Leeds Music, Ltd. (London)	Belwin-Mills
Lehne	Lehne & Co. (Hannover)	
Lemoine	Henri Lemoine & Cie. (Paris)	Presser
Lengnick	Alfred Lengnick & Co., Ltd. Purley Oaks Studios 421a Brighton Road South Croydon, Surrey England	
Lerolle	Lerolle (Paris) (later: Rouart-Lerolle)	
Leuckart	F. E. C. Leuckart (Munich-Leipzig)	Associated
Lienau	Robert Lienau Musikverlag (Berlin)	Peters
Litolff	Collection Litolff (Frankfurt am Main-Leipzig)	Peters
Ludwig	Ludwig Music Publishing Co. 557-67 East 140th Street Cleveland, OH 44110	
Lyche	Harald Lyche & Co. (Oslo)	Peters
McGinnis	McGinnis and Marx Music Publishers (New York)	Deiro
Magnamusic	Magnamusic-Baton, Inc. 10370 Page Industrial Blvd. St. Louis, MO 63132	
ManuscriptPub	Manuscript Publications 219 NW 13th Street Pendleton, OR 97801	

Marx	Josef Marx Music Co. (New York) (later: McGinnis)	
Mathot	A. L. Mathot (Paris) (later: Salabert)	
Maurer	J. Maurer Watermanlaan 7 1150 Brussels, Belgium	
MCA	MCA Music (New York)	Belwin-Mills
Media	Media Press Box 895 Champaign, IL 61820	
Mercier	Mercier (Paris)	
Mercury	Mercury Music Corp.	Presser
Merion	Merion Music, Inc.	Presser
Merrymount	Merrymount Music, Inc.	Presser
Metropolis	Editions Metropolis (Antwerp)	ElkanH
MezhdKniga	Mezhdunarodnaya Kniga (Music Publishers of the USSR)	MCA
Mills	Mills Music Inc. (later: Belwin-Mills)	
Mistetstwo	Mistetstwo, Ukrainischer Verlag Puschkinstrasse 44 Kharkow, USSR *or* Swerdlostrasse Nr. 19 Kiev, USSR	
Mitteldeutscher	Mitteldeutscher Verlag (Halle-Saale)	Peters

Moderne	Edition Moderne Musikverlag Hans Wewerka Franz-Josef-Strasse 2 8 Munich 13, West Germany	
Moeck	Hermann Moeck Verlag (Celle)	Belwin-Mills
Möseler	Möseler Verlag Postfach 460 3340 Wolfenbüttel, West Germany	
Morawe	Morawe & Scheffelt Hochallee 40 Hamburg, West Germany	
Mowbray	Mowbray Music Publishers	Presser
Müller	Willy Müller, Süddeutscher Musikverlag (Heidelberg)	Peters
MüllerF	Fritz Müller (Karlsruhe)	
Muraille	Muraille Veuve Rue des Augustins Liege, Belgium	
Murdoch	I. G. Murdoch & Co. (London)	
Musgis	Musgis, Sowjetischer Zentralverlag (Moscow) (after 1964: Muzyka; later: MezhdKniga)	
Musicus	Edition Musicus, Inc. 333 West 52nd Street New York, NY 10019	
MusPerc	Music for Percussion 17 West 60th Street New York, NY 10023	
MusPr	Music Press	Presser
MusPubHold	Music Publishers Holding Corp.	

MusRara	Musica Rara (London)	Rubank
MusUn	Musik-Union (Frankfurt am Main) (members: Novello, Oxford, Curwen, Williams, Chester)	Boosey
Muzyka	Muzyka, Soviet Central Publishers (Moscow) (later: MezhdKniga)	
Naklada	Muzicka Naklada (Musikverlag des Verbandes der Musikvereinigungen Kroatiens) Opaticka Ulica 10 Zagreb, Yugoslavia	
Neldner	P. Neldner (Riga)	
NewMus	New Music Edition	Presser
NewValley	New Valley Music Press Music Department Smith College Northampton, MA 01063	
Nicosias	Nicosias (Paris)	
Nordiska	A. B. Nordiska Musikförlaget Edition Wilhelm Hansen Pipersgaten 29 Stockholm, Sweden	
NorskKomp	Norsk Komponistforening (Society of Norwegian Composers) Klingenberggaten 5 Oslo, Norway	
Novello	Novello & Co. (London)	Boosey
NYPubLib	The New York Public Library Publications	Peters
Oertel	Louis Oertel Kärntnerplatz 2 Hannover-Waldheim, West Germany	

Okra	Okra Music Corp. (New York)	Seesaw
Omega	Omega Music Company	Fox
Ongaku	Ongaku No Tomo Sha Corp. (Tokyo)	Presser
Orbis	Orbis (Prague)	Artia
Orlando	Orlando-Musikverlag Dachauerstrasse 173 8 Munich 19, West Germany	
OR-TAV	OR-TAV Music Publications P. O. Box 3200 Tel Aviv, Israel	
Ostara	Ostara Press, Inc.	Western
Oxford	Oxford University Press, Inc. 200 Madison Avenue New York, NY 10016	
Panton	Panton (Publishing House of the Czech Music Fund) (Prague)	General
Patelson	Joseph Patelson Music House 160 West 56th Street New York, NY 10019	
Paxton	W. Paxton & Co. (London)	
Peer	Peer International Corp. (New York) (later: Peer-Southern)	
Peer-Southern	Peer-Southern Organization 1740 Broadway New York, NY 10019	
Peters	C. F. Peters Corp. 373 Park Avenue New York, NY 10016	
Petit	Petit (Paris)	

Philippo	Editions Philippo-Combre 24, Boulevard Poissonnière Paris 9, France	
Pleyel	Ignatz Pleyel (Paris)	
Pohl	Pohl-Wohnlich Pierne A. Pohl (Basel-Lörrach)	
Polnischer	Polnischer Staatsverlag (later: PolWydMuz)	
PolWydMuz	Polskie Wydawnictwo Muzyczne (Warsaw)	Belwin-Mills
Presser	Theodore Presser Co. Presser Place Bryn Mawr, PA 19010	
ProArt	Pro Art Publications, Inc. 469 Union Avenue Westbury, NY 11590	
ProMusica	Pro-Musica Verlag (Leipzig)	BroudeA
Rahter	D. Rahter (Hamburg) (later: SimBenjRaht)	
Reinecke	Reinecke Gebrüder (Leipzig)	
Ricard	Ricard	
Ricordi	G. Ricordi & Co. (Milan)	Belwin-Mills
Rideau	Les Editions Rideau Rouge (Paris)	Presser
Ries&Erler	Ries & Erler, Musikverlag (Berlin-Grunewald)	Peters
Rieter	J. Rieter-Biedermann Forsthausstrasse 101 Frankfurt am Main, West Germany	

Robitscheck	Adolf Robitscheck Am Graben 14 Vienna 1, Austria	
Rongwen	Rongwen Music, Inc.	BroudeBr
Rouart	Rouart-Lerolle et Cie. (Paris)	Salabert
Rouhier	Louis Rouhier (Paris)	
Roznyai	Karol Roznyai (Budapest)	
Rozsavölgyi	Rozsavölgyi & Co. (Budapest-Leipzig)	
Rubank	Rubank Inc. 16215 NW 15th Avenue Miami, FL 33169	
Rühle	Karl Rühle (Leipzig-Reudnitz)	
Rushworth	Rushworth & Dreaper (Liverpool)	
RussSt	Russian State Publication Co. (Moscow) (later: Musgis, then Muzyka, then MezhdKniga)	
RussVer	Russische Vereinigung "Internationales Buch" (Moscow)	
SAEM	Societe anonyme d'editions et de musique (Nancy)	
Salabert	Editions Salabert 575 Madison Avenue New York, NY 10022	
Santis	Edizioni de Santis Via Cassia 13 Rome, Italy	
Schirmer	G. Schirmer, Inc. 866 Third Avenue New York, NY 10022	

SchirmerEC	E. C. Schirmer Music Co. 112 South Street Boston, MA 02111	
Schlesinger	Schlesinger (Berlin) (later: Lienau)	
Schmid	Wilhelm Schmid (Leipzig)	
SchmidtAP	Arthur P. Schmidt (Boston-Leipzig)	
SchmidtCF	C. F. Schmidt Cäcilienstrasse 62 Heilbronn/Neckar, West Germany	
Schott	B. Schott's Söhne (Mainz)	EuroAmer
Schott(Brussels)	Schott Frères (Brussels)	Peters
Schott(London)	Schott & Co., Ltd. (London)	EuroAmer
Schuberth	J. Schuberth & Co. Moritzstrasse 39 Wiesbaden, West Germany	
Schweers	Schweers & Haake Mittelstrasse 3 Bremen 1, West Germany	
SDMBrazil	Serviço de Documentação Musical da Ordem dos Músicos do Brasil Av. Almte. Barroso 72-7º Anda Rio de Janeiro, Brazil	
Seeling	J. G. Seeling (Dresden)	
Seesaw	Seesaw Music Corp. 1966 Broadway New York, NY 10023	
Senart	Maurice Senart & Cie. (Paris)	Salabert

Shapiro	Shapiro, Bernstein & Co., Inc. 17 West 60th Street New York, NY 10023	
Shawnee	Shawnee Press, Inc. Delaware Water Gap, PA 18327	
Sieber	Johann Georg Sieber (Paris) (later: Costallat)	
Sikorski	Musikverlag Hans Sikorski (Hamburg)	Belwin-Mills
SimBenjRaht	N. Simrock, A. Benjamin, D. Rahter (Hamburg)	Associated
Simon	Karl Simon (Berlin) (later: Breitkopf)	
Simrock	N. Simrock (Hamburg) (later: SimBenjRaht)	
Sirène	La Sirène musicale (Paris)	
Sirius	Sirius Verlag (Berlin)	Peters
Skandinavisk	Skandinavisk Musikforlag Borgergade 2 Copenhagen, Denmark	
Slovenský	Slovenský Hudobný Fond Gorkého 19 Bratislava, Czechoslovakia	
Sonzogno	Casa Musicale Sonzogno (Turin)	Belwin-Mills
SouthernTX	Southern Music Co., Inc. P. O. Box 329 1100 Broadway San Antonio, TX 78292	
SPAM	Society for the Publication of American Music, Inc.	Presser

Sprague-Coleman	Sprague-Coleman, Inc. 62 West 45th Street New York, NY 10036	
Spratt	Spratt Music Publishers 17 West 60th Street New York, NY 10023	
Stainer	Stainer & Bell, Ltd. (London)	Galaxy
Statni	Statni nakladatelstvi krasne literatury hudby a umeni (Prague)	
Steingräber	Steingräber-Verlag H. Pilz Auf der Reiwiese 9 Offenbach, West Germany *or* Adolfsallee 34 Wiesbaden, West Germany	
Steup	Steup	
Stöppler	Stöppler	
Suecia	Suecia	
Süddeutscher	Süddeutscher Musikverlag (Heidelberg) (*see* Müller)	Peters
Suvini-Zerboni	Edizioni Suvini Zerboni (Milan)	Boosey
Svenska	Föreningen Svenska Tonsättare Tegnerlunden 3 Stockholm, Sweden	
Swan	Swan & Co. (London)	
Templeton	Templeton Publishing Co., Inc.	Shawnee
Tetra	Tetra Music Corp.	BroudeA

Tischer	Tischer & Jagenberg Wilhelmshöhenstrasse 6a Starnberg, West Germany	
Tonos	Edition Tonos (Darmstadt)	EuroAmer
Transatlantiques	Editions Musicales Transatlantiques (Paris)	Presser
Tritone	Tritone Press and Tenuto Publications	Presser
Universal	Universal Edition (London-Vienna)	EuroAmer
UnivNacCuyo	Universidad Nacional de Cuyo (Mendoza)	
UnMusEsp	Union Musical Española (Madrid)	Associated
Urbanek	Fr. A. Urbanek & Söhne (Prague)	
Valley	The Valley Music Press (South Hadley, MA)	
Verband	Verband der tschechoslowakischen Komponisten Prof. Antonin Hyska Neustadt, Sokolska 4/III Prague 2, Czechoslovakia	
VerDeutschTon	Verlagsanstalt deutscher Tonkünstler (Mainz)	
VerMKW	Verlag für musikalische Kultur und Wissenschaft (Wolfenbüttel)	
ViennaUrEd	Vienna Urtext Edition	Schott
Vieweg	Ch. Friedrich Vieweg (Berlin)	Peters
Vincent	Vincent (London)	
Voggenreiter	Voggenreiter-Verlag Meckenheimerstrasse 12 Bad Godesberg-Mehlem, West Germany	

Volkwein	Volkwein Bros., Inc. 117 Sandusky Street Pittsburgh, PA 15212	
Warner	Warner Bros. Music 9200 Sunset Blvd. Los Angeles, CA 90069	
Weinberger	Josef Weinberger (Vienna- Frankfurt-London-Zürich)	Boosey
Western	Western International Music, Inc. 2859 Holt Ave. Los Angeles, CA 90034	
Williams	Joseph Williams Editions (London)	Galaxy
Willis	Willis Music Co. 7380 Industrial Blvd. Florence, KY 41042	
Witmark	Witmark	
Wollenweber	Verlag Walter Wollenweber (Munich)	EuraAmer
Woolhouse	Charles Woolhouse (London)	
Ysaÿe	Editions Ysaÿe (Brussels)	ElkanH
Zanibon	Guglielmo Zanibon (Padua)	Peters
Zenemükiado	Zenemükiado Vallalat (Budapest)	
Zimmermann	Wilhelm Zimmermann (Frankfurt)	Peters

BIBLIOGRAPHY

ALTMANN, Wilhelm. *Kammermusik-Katalog. Ein Verzeichnis von seit 1841 veröffentlichen Kammermusikwerken.* 6th ed. Hofheim am Taunus: Friedrich Hofmeister, 1945.

ALTMANN, Wilhelm, and BORISSOWSKY, WADIM. *Literaturverzeichnis für Bratsche und Viola d'amore. Eine Vollständigkeit anstrebende, auch ungedruckte Werke berücksichtigende Bibliographie.* Wolfenbüttel: Verlag für Musikalische Kultur und Wissenschaft, 1937.

ANDERSON, Robert. "Viola." *Musical Times* 111 (May 1970): 534.

BAKER, Theodore. *Baker's Biographical Dictionary of Musicians.* 5th ed. Edited by Nicolas Slonimsky. New York: G. Schirmer, 1958. Supplements: 1965, 1971.

BARRETT, Henry. *The Viola. Complete Guide for Teachers and Students.* Birmingham, AL: University of Alabama Press, 1972.

BLUME, Friedrich, ed. *Die Musik in Geschichte und Gegenwart.* 14 vols. Kassel: Bärenreiter, 1949-1967. Supplement: 1973.

British Broadcasting Corporation. Central Music Library. *BBC Music Library Chamber Music Catalogue.* London: British Broadcasting Corporation, 1965.

BROOK, Barry S., ed. *The Breitkopf Thematic Catalogue.* Leipzig: Breitkopf & Härtel, 1762-1787; reprint ed., New York: Dover, 1966.

BULL, Storm. *Index to Biographies of Contemporary Composers.* 2 vols. New York and Metuchen, NJ: Scarecrow Press, 1964, 1974.

Centre Belge de Documentation Musicale. *Catalogue des Oeuvres de Compositeurs Belges.* 20 numbers. Brussels: Centre Belge de Documentation Musicale, 1953-1957.

——————. *Music in Belgium: Contemporary Belgian Composers.* Brussels: A. Manteau, 1964.

CHRIST, Peter. *Composium Directory of New Music.* 4 vols. Los Angeles: Crystal Record Company, 1972-1975.

Composers' Guild of Great Britain. *Catalogue of Members' Compositions.* Vol. 1: *British Orchestral Music.* London: Composers' Guild of Great Britain, 1958.

——————. *Catalogue of Members' Compositions.* Vol. 2: *Orchestral Music by Living British Composers.* London: British Music Information Centre, 1970.

EAGON, Angelo. *Catalog of Published Concert Music by American Composers.* 2nd ed. Metuchen, NJ: Scarecrow Press, 1969.

FARISH, Margaret K. *String Music in Print.* 2nd ed. New York: R. R. Bowker, 1973.

GROVE, Sir George, ed. *Grove's Dictionary of Music and Musicians.* 5th ed. Edited by Eric Blom. 9 vols. London: Macmillan, 1954. Supplementary volume, edited by Eric Blom and Denis Stevens, 1966.

GRÜNBERG, Max. *Führer durch die Literatur der Streichinstrumente (Violin, Viola, Violoncello). Kritisches, progressiv geordnetes Repertorium von instruktiven Solo- und Ensemble-Werken.* Leipzig: Breitkopf & Härtel, 1913.

HILL, Frank W. "Music for the Viola." *American String Teacher* 9 (Fall 1959): 27.

LaMARIANA, A. "Music for Viola and Piano." *School Musician* 31 (January 1960): 20 passim.

——————. "Solos for Contest Use." *School Musician* 26 (January 1955): 51-52.

LETZ, Hans. *Music for the Violin and Viola.* The Field of Music, vol. 2.
New York: Rinehart and Company, Inc., 1948.

MOREY, George. *A List of Selected Works for Viola.* Denton, TX: North
Texas State College, 1954.

"Music Received." *Music Library Association Notes.*

NEWMAN, William S. *The Sonata in the Baroque Era.* Chapel Hill, NC:
University of North Carolina Press, 1959.

—————. *The Sonata in the Classic Era.* Chapel Hill, NC: University of
North Carolina Press, 1963.

—————. *The Sonata Since Beethoven.* Chapel Hill, NC: University of
North Carolina Press, 1969.

Pan American Union. Music Section. *Composers of the Americas.*
Washington, DC: Pan American Union, 1955-.

PAZDIREK, Franz. *Universal-Handbuch der Musikliteratur aller Zeiten und
Völker.* 14 vols. Vienna: Pazdirek & Co., 1904-1910. Reprint ed.,
Hilversum: Fritz Knuf, 1966, 12 vols.

RICHTER, Johannes Friedrich. *Kammermusik-Katalog. Verzeichnis der von
1944 bis 1958 veröffentlichen Werke für Kammermusik . . .*
Leipzig: Friedrich Hofmeister, 1960.

RIEMANN, Hugo. *Musik-Lexicon.* 12th ed. Edited by Wilibald Gurlitt.
3 vols. Mainz: B. Schott's Söhne, 1959-1967. Supplements:
2 vols., 1975.

STIERHOF, Karl. "Die Viola und ihre Solo-Literatur." *Oesterreichische
Musik-Zeitschrift* 17 (March 1962): 125-29.

TAYLOR, Roger H. "The Solo Viola Literature of the Classic Period."
American String Teacher 16 (Summer 1967): 15-20

United States Library of Congress. *Library of Congress Catalog, Music and
Phonorecords . . . .* Washington, DC: The Library of Congress, 1954-.

"Viola and Piano." *Music and Letters* 42 (1961): 190-92.

"Viola and Piano." *School Musician* 29 (January 1958): 46.

ZEYRINGER, Franz. *Literatur für Viola. Verzeichnis der Werke für Viola-Solo, Duos mit Viola, Trios mit Viola, Viola-Solo mit Begleitung, Blockflöte mit Viola, Gesang mit Viola, und der Schul- und Studienwerke für Viola.* Hartberg: Julius Schönwetter, 1963. Ergänzungsband, 1965.

——. "Die Viola und ihre Literatur." *Musikerziehung* 19 (1966): 119-23, 157-62.